How to Submit

Praise for *How to Submit*

"A perceptive, inspiring, and practical guide that is also a joyful celebration of one of our best human attributes: the desire to create and share art. Here the necessary process of submitting is treated as a rewarding communal endeavor, rather than as a means to an end. *How to Submit* is an essential companion for any writer seeking to build a literary life."

— **Jennifer Acker**, author of *The Limits of the World* and editor in chief of *The Common*

"The small press ecosystem is a thriving place where dedicated editors and readers provide a habitat for a diversity of authors, both established and up-and-coming. But how to participate? Positive and practical, encouraging and enlightening, Dennis James Sweeney's *How to Submit* offers an essential answer to anyone and everyone seeking to escape the slog of the slush pile and find a home for their work. A field guide written in a firm but friendly voice, Sweeney's vibrant handbook will tell you how to get published, yes, but even more importantly how to get *involved*."

— **Kathleen Rooney**, author of *Where Are the Snows,* editor of Rose Metal Press, and founding member of Poems While You Wait

"For years Dennis James Sweeney performed the generous work of connecting writers and editors through his well-known 'Where to Submit' series. Now he's written a clear, practical, and caring guide to how writers, small presses, and literary magazines may find and sustain one another. This book is an accessible, community-minded resource that will help writers on the path to publication."

— **Hilary Plum**, author of *State Champ*, Open Prose Series editor at Rescue Press, and cohost of *Index for Continuance*

"Chock-full of information, practical advice, and relevant anecdotes, *How to Submit* is an essential resource for writers who want to see their work out in the world. Dennis James Sweeney walks you through every step of the submission process — breaking down its logistical and human layers, and leaving you more grounded and confident about the prospect of submitting. *How to Submit* also compellingly explores the importance of small presses and how writers should engage with them. If you're ready to enter the next stage in your writing journey, or if you've been needing a clear and inspiring refresher guide on submissions, this book is as good as it gets."

— **Dariel Suarez**, author of *The Playwright's House*
and artistic director at GrubStreet

"I wish this book had been available when I started out as a writer so many years ago. It's indispensable. Because it's inspiring. Because it's hands-on useful. Because it captures the essence of why we write and want to share our stories: to find our people, to build a community, to create worlds, to be. If you're the head of an MFA program, give this book as a graduation present to every student. If you're a writer, steal copies of this and give them to all your writing friends. This isn't just a book about submitting and publishing. It's a book that speaks to the very heart of what it means to write."

— **Grant Faulkner**, cofounder of *100 Word Story*
and author of *The Art of Brevity*

"In *How to Submit*, Dennis James Sweeney has crafted a thoughtful and generous map that illuminates the journey from writing to published works. With specific examples, writing prompts, and scads of resources, Sweeney's encouraging guide demystifies the worlds of literary journals and publishers. *How to Submit* is an essential and encouraging tool for anyone who wants their words to find a home in the world, and Sweeney's warmth and generosity shine through every page."

— **Ruth Dickey**, author of *Our hollowness sings*
and executive director of the National Book Foundation

"There are plenty of sources available — online and in print — that provide lists of where to submit your writing; this guide explains *how* to submit. Dennis James Sweeney brings together case studies and his own experiences as an author and teacher to help writers find more success with their writing. This book has it all."

— **Robert Lee Brewer**, editor of *Writer's Market*
and senior editor of *Writer's Digest*

How to Submit

Getting Your Writing Published with Literary Magazines and Small Presses

DENNIS JAMES SWEENEY

New World Library
Novato, California

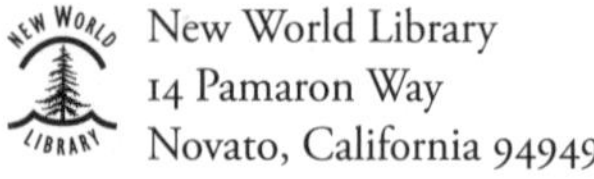
New World Library
14 Pamaron Way
Novato, California 94949

Text design by Tona Pearce Myers

Library of Congress Cataloging-in-Publication Data

Names: Sweeney, Dennis James, author.
Title: How to submit : getting your writing published with literary magazines and small presses / Dennis James Sweeney.
Description: Novato, California : New World Library, [2025] | Includes index. | Summary: "*How to Submit* is the essential guide to publishing your writing with literary magazines and small presses. Providing writers with the tools and guidance to successfully submit their writing, *How to Submit* is also a manifesto for finding community and inspiration in the process of publication"-- Provided by publisher.
Identifiers: LCCN 2024048213 (print) | LCCN 2024048214 (ebook) | ISBN 9781608689361 (trade paperback) | ISBN 9781608689378 (epub)
Subjects: LCSH: Authorship--Marketing. | Publishers and publishing.
Classification: LCC PN161 .S94 2025 (print) | LCC PN161 (ebook) | DDC 808.02--dc23/eng/20241122
LC record available at https://lccn.loc.gov/2024048213
LC ebook record available at https://lccn.loc.gov/2024048214

First printing, February 2025
ISBN 978-1-60868-936-1
Ebook ISBN 978-1-60868-937-8
Printed in Canada

10 9 8 7 6 5 4 3 2 1

New World Library is committed to protecting our natural environment. This book is made of material from well-managed FSC®-certified forests and other controlled sources.

Contents

Introduction

A famous young writer once visited my MFA program in Oregon. A few years earlier, she had published a short story collection that won several prestigious prizes and was passed around with awe among the writers in my workshop. Now she was touring on behalf of her debut novel. This writer burst into our quiet, often humble writing program with all the flair of a person who didn't have to prove anything to anyone, especially us.

Her first event on campus was a graduate students–only session, in which the students sat lined at a series of long tables. The writer sat on a table at the front. She said she was going to be honest with us. She would tell us the story of how she got where she was, because we deserved to know how things worked.

The writer, like us, had attended a funded MFA program. Like us, she had worked on short stories there. The difference arose when one of the writer's short stories caught her professor's attention. The professor forwarded that story to an editor at a famous magazine. The magazine published it. An agent read the story, contacted the writer, and signed her. The writer finished her collection, and the agent sold it. She told us the number of her advance. We gasped.

"In conclusion," the writer said, "I have never submitted to the slush pile."

We groaned. Or we held in our groans, because at least she had been honest with us.

But her honesty hurt. The story was all so achingly true. My classmates and I sat there feeling hamstrung, the whole discouraged lot of us.

We were submitting our writing. *We* had dreams of getting published. But the writer had shared the reality of a literary fame we could only dream of. Now we understood its angles, its improbability. We couldn't help but resent the writer's generous act of sharing her story — well, *I* couldn't help but resent it.

That was because I hadn't yet grasped an essential fact about publishing: there is another way, and that way can be even more rewarding than the famous writer's.

• • •

This book is about that other way. This way involves submitting to the "slush pile," yes. But I don't call it the slush pile. I call it finding a home for your writing.

Submitting to literary magazines and small presses is an essential way to achieve your publishing goals. It is writer led, community based, and accessible. Submitting your writing means entering a vibrant landscape of readers, writers, and editors who have devoted their energy to the written word. To submit is to participate in the feat of building this space together. It is an act of community.

I believe in that community and its possibilities, which is why I wrote *How to Submit*.

This book is for everyone sitting in the room with the famous writer, wondering how we're going to get published. It is for everyone who wants to share our work with others, and who wants to take that process into our own hands. It is for everyone in search of a community where not only our writing but also we ourselves belong.

More specifically, this book is about how to submit your writing without an agent advocating for you. It is about how to be published without the machinery of the Big 5 publishers (Penguin Random House, HarperCollins, Macmillan, Hachette, and Simon & Schuster) — how to be published, instead, under the steam of your own desire, your relationship with your writing, and your participation in the literary landscape. It is about finding people who treat your book not as a business but as the dream that it is, as the light that only you can bring into the world.

There's nothing wrong with the famous writer's publication story. By now my resentment has given way to the conviction that everyone has their own path. Every path is valid and meaningful, including the famous writer's. But her path — to an agent and a Big 5 publisher — is where how-to books about publishing usually lead.

That's why *How to Submit* is so necessary. Many of us walk the path of submitting our writing, and yet that path is rarely celebrated. I want to give the act of submitting to literary magazines and small presses the attention it deserves.

For most of us, publication is a journey. It involves rejection, uncertainty, and long hours of labor, with no clear result. I am here to tell you that, if you keep working, you will find the right place — the right community — for your writing. Doing so is a matter of time and energy, yes, but also of passion, purpose, soul-searching, patience, and generosity toward every reader, editor, and writer involved in the process, including *you*.

You'll find your way to share your writing. This book is meant to help.

• • •

My own story began fifteen years ago in my parents' basement. The summer after I graduated from college, I sat at my grandpa's narrow desk, typing what I thought would be my first novel. By the end of the first page, I was thinking about publication. I was obsessed with the idea that I had something to say, and that I might be able to share it.

The novel didn't work out, which made sense, given that I had just begun my relationship with creative writing. But I kept working, turning my attention to short stories I could finish. I began submitting stories when I moved to Taipei at the end of that summer. I remember sitting on my thin mattress on the floor, polishing my sentences over and over before winging stories out to magazines I had just discovered.

They didn't take at first. I received rejection after rejection, which I quickly learned was the norm. But I kept trying. A few months later, to my amazement, the online magazine *elimae* accepted a series of flash fictions I had written.

I couldn't believe it. People would read my stories! Not only that, but *elimae* was a publication I had come to know and respect. Its simple design and excitingly weird writing resonated with my off-kilter taste, and now I would see my own work in it. The day my stories went live felt like a quiet but firm beginning.

In the year that followed, I set out on a backpacking journey across Southeast Asia, India, and Nepal. I committed myself to writing every day in a set of notebooks friends and family had given me. In Bali I transcribed an excerpt from my handwritten journal at a web café, then submitted it, all in the same hourly internet session. In Auroville, an intentional community in South India, I bought a computer from a fellow traveler and revised my short stories on the thatched floor of our communal hut. On the Annapurna Circuit, a one-hundred-mile trail through the Himalayas, I wrote poems that traced the energy of each day's hike, even as my body approached the edge of exhaustion.

When I returned to the United States, I moved to Boulder, Colorado, and found a job as a cashier at a natural foods store. I spent most of my mornings huddled in my basement apartment, writing linked short prose pieces before going in to work the evening shift. A chapbook of fictional prose poems, *What They Took Away*, emerged from these writing sessions. Like so much of what I wrote, I submitted it.

Months later, I received an email from *CutBank*, the University of Montana's literary magazine and the publishers of their chapbook series. The email began, "Congratulations!" *What They Took Away* had won their contest. It was to be published early the next year as a perfect-bound chapbook.

My response to *CutBank*'s acceptance letter reads:

> What??????? Really?????? That is the best news I've ever heard. Oh my goodness. Wow. Yes, the chapbook is still available.
>
> Just a question, for now: Is this really true? The chapbook is out in one other contest and just want to confirm before I withdraw it from their consideration. I really can't believe it.
>
> You have no idea how much this means. Or maybe you do…
>
> Thank you!

I was elated. I was going to have an actual, real-life book to my name. The chapbook was published the next spring, complete with a cover from Odilon Redon, a symbolist painter whose drawings I had found in the public domain, and a blurb from one of my favorite indie hybrid writers. I traveled to Seattle for the AWP writers conference the month the book was published. I gave the first literary reading of my life. I was nervous as hell, standing in front of an audience that seemed to know far more than me about how these things went. I held my book in my hand. It was so thin but so real.

Since then, submitting my work has been far from smooth sailing. I have received countless rejections, regularly reevaluated my writing, and even questioned my drive to pursue publication. But along the way, I have also received enough acceptances to make me imagine, maybe, that I actually *am* a part of this literary landscape, that I actually *do* have the capacity to write something that will affect someone.

The literary magazines and small presses I've worked with run the gamut of size, focus, and funding. They include tiny experimental poetry magazines, online flash fiction stalwarts, and one-person publishers of hand-stapled, folded-paper chapbooks. They also include university-funded literary journals, a major national newspaper, and storied independent presses whose authors have gone on to win prestigious awards.

I have learned to tone it down a little in my replies to editors' emails, but the thrill of acceptance never quite goes away. In the moment of publication, it feels like the work has come full circle. Writing always begins, for me, with a deep need to communicate. When it arrives in the world, it's as if that act of communication has finally reached its home.

The more I write, the more I realize my writing has always begun with that premise: I want to share this with someone.

• • •

But who is that someone? This is the first question we should ask, but often don't, when it comes to submitting our writing. Finding my audience — my community — is the other half of my writing journey, a parallel journey you don't often hear about, which has as much to do with my publications as my writing itself.

Early in my writing life, I fantasized that my career path would follow that of the famous authors I was reading. I would work hard and write great books, yes. But everything after that would just *happen*: a generalized flock of admiring readers would eventually take to my work and make me famous. Who were the readers? They were just *out there*. I never imagined their faces. I didn't think I had to.

The more I wrote, however, the more I found myself hungry for community. I wanted to know where my writing belonged. I wanted to know where *I* belonged. I remembered how lonely and decontextualized writing had felt when I began my failed novel in my parents' basement. That kind of writing simply wasn't sustainable for me.

So I began to search. While I lived in Taiwan, I read through literary magazines online and checked out the books on the English language bookshelves at the Taipei library. I discovered Don DeLillo and Haruki Murakami and Roberto Bolaño, all writers who impressed me and, at the same time, seemed to speak from a magisterial distance. They wrote as if from the other side of an unachievable literary dream.

Then one day, on those same bookshelves, I found a copy

of Amelia Gray's *AM/PM*. Compared to the tomes I had been reading, *AM/PM* felt friendly and authentic. Its cover was a hand-drawn sketch, its pages filled with loosely linked flash fictions that were generous and funny and, most of all, *open*. Like the online literary magazines I had recently discovered, *AM/PM* made it feel possible to be a writer.

I couldn't help writing a short email to Amelia Gray telling her how much the book meant to me. Amazingly, she responded. When she received my message, she wrote, she was sitting next to one of the publishers at a wedding, and she shared the email with them. Hearing back from her felt like a confirmation of what I experienced reading her book. It felt like leaving my small square room and stepping into a community.

By the time I returned to the United States, I had followed that spirit into the landscape of indie publishing. Through social media, internet searching, and my ongoing reading, I began to understand more about the small press and literary magazine scene. My desire to connect with other writers led me to *HTMLGIANT*, an edgy literary site at the juxtaposition of innovative writing and indie publishing communities. I reached out to the reviews editor, Janice Lee, offering to review books if there were any that needed reviewing.

I had never written a book review before, but I ended up writing thirteen of them over the year that followed. I was hungry to read and hungry to be a part of the conversation. When *HTMLGIANT* shut down, Janice contacted me about being a part of a new literary website, *Entropy*. I reviewed more books for *Entropy*, and soon Janice asked if I might be interested in being the small press editor for the site.

That's when I took over the "Where to Submit" list, which Janice herself had begun. Every three months, I compiled a list of every press and literary magazine I could find that were accepting submissions. The more I researched, the more the list expanded, and soon it became a popular hub for writers looking to send out their work. Its popularity surprised me, although it shouldn't have. I was the same as every writer who used the list: eager for a resource that would help me decide what to do with my writing.

During this time, I moved to Oregon to begin my MFA in creative writing. Meeting other writers and reading their works in progress was a revelation to me. I had a hard time listening to feedback on my stories, but I liked being in a place where we were all there for the writing, this quixotic thing we cared about deeply. Meeting other writers in person, not just through the internet, gave a real-life dimension to the work I had been doing.

After I graduated, I felt the need for even more connection. I loved the people I met in Oregon, but my MFA program had been relatively separate from the writing and reading communities I was participating in online. I wanted to go to a place where those communities met. The University of Denver's PhD program in creative writing sounded like that place. I applied and, astoundingly to me, was accepted. I moved to Denver.

That was where the worlds I had been inhabiting came together. I had encountered so many of the writers in Denver on the internet, in books, through *Entropy* or social media, and now they were here in real life. We shared reference points, contexts, and histories of reading and thinking. We believed in innovative writing and pressing against the status quo. We believed in the space between genres where work that was hard to name lived and flourished. Many of us contributed to the writing community as much as we benefited from it, publishing and supporting others whose work we admired.

All of a sudden — or perhaps not all of a sudden but after almost a decade of reading and interacting — my sense of who I was writing for had changed. My "audience" wasn't a mass of faceless readers. It was, instead, the community that I had come to be a part of over these years. It was less an audience, in fact, than a conversation. Everything I wrote was part of that conversation. Together we were writing our community into being.

This sense of community is something I will return to throughout this book. It is like a compass for me: the conviction that there are people out there who want to connect with your work as much as you want to connect with them. These people aren't passive recipients of your writing. They're not "buyers."

They're your community, whether or not you've found them yet. They're in conversation with you already. They're not *they*; they're us.

• • •

This book brings two halves of the conversation together: the writer and the reader. The work and the community where the work belongs. I firmly believe that the process of submitting and publishing works best when it doesn't feel primarily like a business arrangement. Small presses and literary magazines make this possible. We meet in that place where passion is the driver, where the work is a form of collective magic.

There are many stages to finding your readers and your community. This book is meant to be helpful during each of them, from the writer who's writing their first stories, essays, or poems to the writer who's been submitting for years.

Here are a few things *How to Submit* can do for you:

- **If you are a beginning writer, it will help you gain a sense of the publishing landscape you are writing within.** As Matthew Salesses argues in *Craft in the Real World*, understanding your audience is essential to the choices you make as a writer. Knowing who you are writing for has everything to do with what and how you write. This book will help you envision your audience, providing an introduction to the landscape of literary magazine and small press publishing as well as advice on how to find the communities that resonate with you as a writer.
- **If you have stories, essays, or poems you are ready to send out, this book will help you decide how to submit them.** Have you written something you like and want to share with the world, but you don't quite know how to seek publication? This book will help you take the difficult step from finished piece to published piece. It will also encourage you to *enjoy* the process of submitting. Sending out your work should energize your writing, not take energy away from it.
- **If you have been submitting for a while but still have questions, this book will support your ongoing work toward publication.** You're not alone if you've been submitting for a while but still have uncertainties and questions. When you're engaged in submitting your work, support and conversation are essential. My hope is that this book will be a resource for all of us who wonder, "Am I doing it right? How do *you* submit your writing?"
- **If you are trying to remind yourself why to send out your writing, this book will encourage you to continue.** *How to Submit* is not just a practical guide.

It is also an argument for the vitality, excitement, and expansiveness of submitting your work. Submitting can be a grind at times, so it's essential to remember the passion that editors, writers, and readers put into cocreating the literary world. This book is meant to remind you of this passion and to allow it to inspire you.

- **If you already have an understanding of the large press publishing world, this book will expand your horizons.** There are plenty of good books about how to get an agent and a book deal (see appendix B). This book talks about publishing less as a "deal" than as an act of community and connection. I wrote *How to Submit* to give back to the writing communities that have supported me, doing my part to illuminate the importance of small presses and literary magazines in the literary landscape as a whole.

I've lived through many of the above stages. *How to Submit* emerges from years of submissions, rejections, and (magically) acceptances, all of which were defined by me flying by the seat of my pants, hoping I was doing it right. There's nothing wrong with that! But my trial-and-error approach was due in large part to the fact that information about publishing is often vague, conversational, or ambient and therefore inaccessible to those who aren't already involved in it. This book is meant to make those conversations more available.

The truth, of course, is that there is no "right" way to submit. I don't have all the answers, and I can't give you a secret key to publication. What I can do is ask the right questions, leading toward your own answers. The point of this book is *your* journey as a submitter. *How to Submit* will help you think about the main problems that arise in submitting your writing, then share strategies and tools that help you navigate them.

This book emerges from a course I taught for several years at GrubStreet, the community writing workshop in Boston. There are so many of us, I learned while teaching this class, who want to share our writing but are daunted by the sheer breadth of magazines, presses, and submission opportunities, not to mention the vulnerable work of asking someone to consider our writing for publication. This book aims to give both guidance and support in the difficult process of submitting your writing.

My students at GrubStreet have been essential to this book, asking questions and sharing stories that have shaped my approach. They are the reason I wrote *How to Submit*: to try to replicate those powerful moments we shared at the end of class, when we had gone from a group of individual writers working on our own projects to a community of writers engaged in the shared goal of publishing our writing.

At its best, submitting becomes just such an act of community. It connects people with intertwining goals and experiences, and it allows us to join the vibrant conversation that precedes us. It allows us to find each other. It also allows us to find ourselves. It reminds us why we were writing all along: to feel that spark of connection when someone hears our writing and we hear theirs and we realize, in a flash of recognition, that we are home.

This book is about entering — and helping to build — the spaces where that kind of connection can happen. *How to Submit* is your guide not just to publication but to learning where your writing belongs.

1

Why to Submit

The first thing to ask yourself when beginning to submit is, Why am I submitting? Your answer to this question will be a guide to your submissions process, helping you decide where, what, and how to submit as well as your long-term strategy for publication. You cannot know *how* to submit until you know *why*.

So before we begin with the logistics and practical stuff, I'm going to ask you to do some soul-searching:

Writing Prompt

Get out your journal and take ten to fifteen minutes to respond to the following questions.

Why do you want to submit your writing? What is your goal, purpose, and/or hope for submitting and publishing your creative work?

I have encountered an illuminating variety of answers to this question in my time teaching classes on how to submit. Writers often have multiple interwoven goals, the spirit of which runs the gamut from curious to hopeful to altruistic, from hesitant to proud to practical. All responses are valid, and all of them are good reasons to work toward publication.

Here is a short list of some of the motivations students have shared:

- To share an important story that you don't see represented enough (or at all).
- To make an impact on your audience, whether the impact is entertainment, edification, or an emotional response.
- To find out if it's good. Are other people interested in your work?
- As a natural evolution of self-expression. As one of my students said, "It just felt like that's what happens next."
- As something to aim for — it keeps you writing.
- Because you're in a generative phase, and writing feels circular without an end goal.
- Because you want to connect with people and find community.
- "Why not?"
- As a challenge: to actually share the writing you've been working on.
- As a sign that you are taking writing seriously, legitimizing (to yourself or others) how you spend your time.
- To build your résumé; for career reasons.
- "To find meaning in the chaos."

- "Fame, glory, and money." (This was said half-jokingly.)
- To honor the work you're doing.
- To satisfy the need for validation: to receive recognition, to be heard.

The funny thing is, the last bullet point often pops up *after* all the others. Many of us are comfortable sharing motivations that seem noble, smart, or thoughtfully linked to the writing process. But it can be hard to share our desire to receive validation from the world.

It can be hard, that is, to admit we need someone to tell us our writing is good and that the thing we love to do is worthwhile. When we submit our writing, we open ourselves to the possibility that this kind of validation might be withheld. It's safer not to take the risk. It's easier to give up the desire to be seen, heard, and known.

But I'm here to tell you to stick with that desire. Wanting validation for your work is not only a reasonable consequence of writing but, for many of us, an essential motivation. Writing is labor, and it deserves recognition.

Let's say you're a woodworker. You spend hours, weeks, and months building chairs. You've worked for years to get the angles right, to figure out the exact arrangement that will make the person who sits in the chair feel good. It started as a hobby, but now it's more. Now it's the thing that gives your life meaning.

Since you've been doing it for a while, you're finally creating chairs you believe in. They're chairs you love, chairs that could fill a house. The problem is, your chairs are all piled up in a shed. No one has seen them besides a few close friends and fellow carpenters. You know they might be just right for someone's home, or for a school or library. They're just sitting there, and you know they could do more.

Wouldn't you want someone to sit in your chairs? Wouldn't you feel totally fine about wanting to share them?

Your writing is like a chair. You've worked hard on it, you've put your heart into it, and now you want someone to experience the results of your passion. For many of us, the desire to share our work is built into the work.

It's essential to hold on to that feeling, since it keeps us in touch with the energy and desire behind the difficult work of submitting our writing.

• • •

My own motivations for submitting have evolved over the years. When I first dreamed of being published, I wanted "fame, glory, and money," in a surprisingly unironic way. I had read books and seen their authors get attention for sharing the depths of their souls. I thought it would satisfy me to become an author. To be read, to be publicly known.

As soon as I got a few pages into my attempted novel, though, I learned that this level of exposure wasn't in the cards anytime soon. I simply hadn't practiced enough to write the novel I wanted to write. That was when I turned my attention to publishing short stories, essays, and poems with literary magazines, which still gave me the kind of attention and validation I was looking for. I experienced a joy and recognition when my writing was accepted that I had never encountered before.

The feeling was addicting. As I wrote more, I found myself submitting like a gambler, sure that if I played enough, I would hit it big. I stayed connected to my writing, but sometimes that connection faltered. I sent out work that wasn't ready. I tried to publish everything I wrote, even when I knew it wouldn't make the cut.

Over the years, I slowly became aware that the thrill of acceptance was never enough. It wasn't reliable or certain, for one thing. More than that, my results-oriented mentality was built on the assumption that what other people thought about my writing was more important than what *I* thought about it. I began to long for the depth of creative engagement I saw in my favorite writers. Their committed attitude led them to focus on their writing for the sake of the work itself. If, finally, they did pursue publication, they did so not as a culmination but as an afterthought.

What I wanted, I realized, was to make a home in my writing. *I* wanted to be the one who decided whether it was good enough.

So I turned toward myself. I built my writing into a refuge. I continued submitting, yes, but I became less and less tied to the result.

That was about the time I finished my PhD program in creative writing. Suddenly I found myself needing a job. I'd also gotten married, and we were thinking about having a baby, which lent a new urgency to my writing career. I decided I needed to get my writing published, fast. The need to prove myself as a writer became an external journey rather than the internal one I'd traced for so long.

I took on a whole new attitude toward submissions. I shaped up books I had been working on for years and developed strategic plans for submitting them. I revived essays that had never quite landed with a literary magazine but that I had always believed in. I selected the writing I wanted to publish, and I took a firm stance: I would not stop working on each piece until it was accepted and appeared in print.

This approach was a revelation for me. My first full-length book was accepted, then my second, then my third. My shorter writing began to be published much more regularly. The systematic energy I brought to the process wasn't my favorite kind to inhabit. But it was solid, in a way that my submissions never had been. I didn't waver because I wasn't submitting exclusively for me anymore.

Only recently have I begun to understand that validation for my writing still means a lot to me. But it is a different kind of validation than I was seeking at the beginning of my writing life. Before, I had cast about for any recognition, any sign from the universe. I wanted to know that what I wrote mattered. Now I've developed an internal strength I was missing earlier. As strange as it feels to say it, I *know* my words matter. I have written enough, and left enough of my writing aside, to have faith in the projects I continue to work on. My writing is meaningful. It does something nobody else's writing does.

With that knowledge, I can take the submission process less personally. Publication becomes a matter not of shoring up my self-confidence but of being recognized for what I already believe in. A "no" to my work feels like someone else's problem, not mine. Rejection is a statement of differing priorities.

That said, I'm still a chair maker. I want someone to use what I have built. My desire to communicate has driven my writing since the beginning, and it still does. Now it's just a matter of finding the people, the publications, and the communities that connect with this act of communication.

• • •

Why, then, should you look for a home in the small press world? Why submit your writing to literary magazines? Why read *How to Submit*? These are important questions, since there are many forking paths to publication.

When it comes to book-length writing, publishing with a small press is sometimes understood as a second choice. You might hear the story of someone who sent their work to agent after agent, only to receive a chorus of rejections and eventually to publish their work with a small press. Or perhaps they found an agent, but that agent wasn't able to sell the book to a major house, so they turned to small presses. These narratives frame small presses as hierarchically below the Big 5 publishers.

Margot Atwell of Feminist Press noticed a similar dynamic when observing the trial in which Penguin Random House tried to purchase rival publisher Simon & Schuster. Throughout the trial, publishing executives referred to small presses as "farm teams" for the large houses. This dismissive description of small presses, Atwell writes in *Lit Hub*, implies not only that small press publishing is at a lower level than that of the Big 5 but also that a small press's primary function is to cultivate talent for the large, corporate publishers.

This equates money and size with value, Atwell argues. But the reality is much different. In Atwell's words, "Independent presses often lack the money to provide authors with higher advances *because* we take risks on work that is more experimental and pushes boundaries — books written by writers who are BIPOC, trans, queer, disabled, neuroatypical, immigrants, or in other ways marginalized by mainstream society and mainstream publishing. We often publish work that has less obvious 'commercial appeal' to serve our missions and enrich the literary landscape." This essential work is only possible in a publishing framework that does not treat profitability as the determining factor in whose writing is published.

Janice Lee put it another way in a *Vol. 1 Brooklyn* article that recounts her experience of searching for a publisher for her novel *Imagine a Death*. After encountering repeated rejections from agents who liked the book but believed it wouldn't sell, she returned to the small press community she had been a prominent part of for years. She had already published several small press books and served as founding editor of *Entropy* and a publisher of the small press Civil Coping Mechanisms. Now, as Lee puts it, she had to align her radical ideas about publishing with her publishing practice itself. She had to let go of wanting to "win the game" of a hierarchical publishing framework. She had to let go of the internalized value she placed on authors with more commercial success. She had to change her idea of what success was.

As an alternative, Lee imagines a nonhierarchical, nonlinear framework for thinking about publishing. She asks, "How would things be different if we thought of books, not as products or commodities, but as bridges? If instead of agonizing about the limits of the self...we moved toward an internal language for shared humanity and interconnectedness? If instead of possession and ownership and separation, we moved towards intimacy, forgiveness, and emancipation?" What if, in other words, we understood small press publishing as an opportunity to think newly about what literature *is*?

For many of us, small presses embody the ideals that brought us to writing in the first place: generosity, shared stories, and horizontal (rather than hierarchical) connection. I won't speak for you, but for me, this is why books glowed when I first fell in love with them. Reading has always given me an experience of quiet but fierce shared language, where it is possible to imagine new ways of thinking about our lives. Books were a refuge from the requirement to *get* something, to *do* something, to *achieve* something in order to be worthwhile. Being in a story was enough.

By building frameworks outside the ones that ordered my

life, books allowed me to see through the false binary of success and failure. They gave me a new sense of presence and connection. They allowed me to imagine other worlds into being. Why not reflect that experience in publishing?

• • •

There are reasons to publish with small presses, of course, beyond these ideals. Practicality and strategy are an equally important part of the picture when deciding where to publish.

One factor that will influence your decision about where to publish is the genre of your writing itself. Novels and narrative nonfiction have an established place in both the Big 5 and the small press landscapes, for example. For other writers, small press publishing is simply the only option, since the Big 5 rarely consider their work.

This is very much the case with poetry. While the classics, and a handful of established poets, are published by the large houses, the vast majority of poetry in the United States is published by small presses. This is part of what makes the poetry world so diverse and open to innovation. Even the most prestigious and prizewinning poetry collections are the product of publishing setups that don't depend exclusively on profiting from their books.

The same goes for most experimental writing. Styles born in innovative writing communities do sometimes break into the mainstream, but they usually emerge from the small press landscape. With my first three books, for example, I didn't even consider querying agents. I knew the publishers that would support their cross-genre approaches would be part of the same small press community that inspired the books.

Similarly, your specific writing goals might motivate you

to publish with a small press. If you want to find community through publishing, a small press may help you access your community most directly. If you want motivation to keep writing, the submission and publication processes I talk about in this book may be the most inspiring for your continued work. If you want validation, a small press might be well-equipped to give you the personalized attention you are looking for.

All this works even if you are coming to small presses after trying for the Big 5. Maybe you queried agents for months or years with a book you thought you could sell. Maybe you got a few bites on your query, but everyone said, "It's a hard market" or "I'll step aside for another agent who is a better fit for the book." Maybe you come to small press publishing wondering whether your book will find a home.

Regardless of how submitting fits in your writing journey, the important thing is to recognize that publishing with a small press is a choice, not a fallback. It's a community, an ecosystem, a whole experience of sharing your work. Entering that experience can be as thrilling, and as much a part of the creative process, as the writing itself.

• • •

Literary magazines are also part of this ecosystem. They carve out a space for poems, essays, and short stories without requiring commercial appeal. They make shorter writing an essential part of the literary conversation, fueling the profusion of writerly possibilities. They act as vibrant bridges between writers and the rest of the world.

There are myriad literary magazines out there — even more than there are presses. Some are well-known stalwarts of contemporary literature with full mastheads and paid staff. Others are student-run endeavors funded by MFA programs in creative writing. Others are run by a few people on mostly volunteer labor, and they preserve all the quirk and solidity of their independence in what they publish.

In terms of their publishing practices, some literary magazines might be invested in ideas of prestige and conventional success. Others might embrace risk, be run on a shoestring budget, and pride themselves in flipping the bird to mainstream publishing. Many keep going for years on the strength of a single passionate editor's labor. They might have weird names, uneven publication schedules, and personal idiosyncrasies. Lit mags are as eclectic and varied as the people who run them. This diversity makes publishing with literary magazines a dynamic, flexible, and ever-renewing experience.

Even a single issue of a literary magazine can be wonderfully varied. Unpublished writers are featured alongside writers with multiple books. Experimental writing appears beside traditional work. Contributors are old and young, published by both small and large presses. Literary magazines create space for conversations between writers that might not otherwise find themselves in the same room.

All this variation means there are many different reasons for publishing in literary magazines. So why should *you* publish in literary magazines? What goals or hopes might motivate you to submit?

A first major reason to submit to literary magazines is their accessibility to writers. It's conceivable, and it happens, that an unpublished, unagented writer could see their first published story, essay, or poem in a well-known national journal. A publication like this could very well arrive through the submissions queue, since almost all literary magazines are at least occasionally open to writers sending their work. Additionally, hundreds of less prestigious venues regularly publish short stories, essays, and poems, which makes your chances of receiving an acceptance relatively high. Because lit mags publish so many writers in a single issue, and because there are more lit mags than presses, they are a major wellspring for new writing. You can submit to them easily as long as you have access to a computer, an internet connection and, at times, a small submission fee.

This makes literary magazines the ideal venue for writers looking to find their place in the literary landscape. Since they feed into both Big 5 publishing models and the small press community, literary magazines are a garden of forking paths. You can send to venues that span different styles, sensibilities, and reading communities on your way to deciding how you want your publishing life to look.

Another good thing about publishing in literary magazines is that it helps you build a reputation, for lack of a better word. You can decide what *reputation* means to you, but for me it has meant slowly being recognized among different communities of writers — and, in turn, reading their work and becoming familiar with them. Publishing with literary magazines also gives you publishing credits, which can act as proof of your accomplishments as a writer. Over time, readers and fellow writers might reach out to tell you they like your work. Editors might even solicit your writing.

Literary magazine submissions can also help you structure your efforts as a writer. Picking a magazine to submit to allows you to set a goal, meet it, and move on. Externally imposed deadlines — many journals open in the fall and close in the spring, for example — allow you to approach your work rhythmically rather than getting lost in the question of what to revise when. If you are writing a full-length book, which is usually a yearslong process, publishing excerpts or other short pieces in literary magazines can also give you regular feedback during the journey to finishing your manuscript.

Perhaps the most rewarding aspect of publishing with literary magazines is the opportunity to share your work alongside a group of other writers. The joy in this can be as simple as flipping through a contributor copy of a literary magazine and discovering exciting new writers in its pages. You can bask in the beauty of the printed (or digital) object and share it with friends and family. You might also form unexpected connections: a relationship with an editor blooms into a friendship, or a fellow contributor reaches out to you and starts a collaboration. Anything can happen when you put your writing out there.

These connections, at best, give back to your writing. They inspire. They build the community where your writing — and you — will land.

• • •

As you use *How to Submit*, I encourage you to keep returning to the question of *why*. It is easy to get lost in the sauce, as they say — to become overwhelmed by the number of opportunities and the vexing process of trying to find a place in the literary world. You can get so involved in trying to get published that you forget why you're doing it.

Stay in touch with what publication means to you. Remember what you want submitting to do for your writing. Then allow these motivations to guide your decision-making about not only *where* to submit (see chapter 2) but also *how* to submit (see chapter 4) and how to engage with editors after acceptance (see chapter 8). Let your writing come full circle. Let submitting fill you up and make your writing even livelier, even more engaged with its contexts, than it was before you sent it out into the world.

2

Where to Submit

When I first took over *Entropy*'s "Where to Submit" list, I didn't know how big of a resource it would become. I was simply continuing Janice Lee's work by compiling a list of the small presses and literary magazines that were open for submissions during a given season. The original lists featured thirty or forty venues. They were not so much comprehensive lists as a guide to our little corner of the literary world.

In the next few years, however, the list grew rapidly. As it grew, more and more writers shared the link on social media. Over time the seasonal arrival of "Where to Submit" became an online event. Writers treated the list as an opportunity to kick-start (or restart) their submissions in the company of others who were doing the same. It was a chance for writers to make sense of the overwhelming number of presses and magazines out there and to see them all in one place, laid out by a trusted source with deadlines, genres, and links to submission guidelines right on the page.

But it wasn't only writers who needed the resource. Once we established the list as a regular offering, literary magazines and small presses began contacting me. Soon my inbox was flooded with requests from editors to list their open reading periods. This is how "Where to Submit" ended up featuring hundreds of venues instead of the tens it began with. During the years I assembled the list, I heard from hundreds of presses and magazines who otherwise would never have been on my map.

It struck me then, and it still strikes me now, how much energy and inspiration went into running each of the literary magazines and small presses featured on the list. Every editor who sent me a listing had immersed themselves in the devotional project of finding and publishing new writing. These editors wanted to get the word out to writers as much as writers wanted to learn about submitting to them.

The connective space of the "Where to Submit" list helped me realize how committed both writers and editors are to the submissions process, and how helpful it can be to have a place where they come together. Luckily, *Entropy* is not the only place where such a listing arose. Numerous writers, editors, and institutions have created resources to help you determine where to submit. You're not alone on this journey.

The literary landscape can be overwhelming, and these resources will help you narrow down the field. My goal in this chapter is to help you search for your people — your small presses, your literary magazines, your editors. They are out there, and you'll find each other soon enough.

• • •

Three different types of resources will help you find submission venues. *Ranked lists* organize publications hierarchically, estimating each venue's relative level of prestige. *Unranked lists* provide a broader view of the many venues for submission, organizing publications using tags and categories instead of prestige. *Getting involved*, which is less a resource than a practice, is the most long-term of these options, since it means building relationships with publication venues over time and learning about their suitability for your work through those relationships.

Ranked Lists

Ranked lists arrange publications from top to bottom, hierarchically. Even if you're not interested in prestige or conventional success, these lists can be a helpful tool for understanding where you are submitting. Prestige works as an engine for everything from response times to selectiveness to the resources and staff a publication is working with, so it will affect your publication experience, regardless of your goals.

It's good to recognize that there is no objective best, and that these resources calculate prestige solely on the basis of their specific criteria. They can't give you the final answer on where to submit. Instead, I think of them as a public service that allows writers to gain a quick familiarity with the reputation of the most well-known publications.

For literary magazines, the two most reliable rankings are maintained by writers who have decided to share their own processes for determining where to submit:

- **Clifford Garstang's Literary Magazine Rankings.** Clifford Garstang uses a by-the-numbers method to rank literary magazines by their number of inclusions and honorable mentions in the Pushcart Prize anthology over the past ten years. Garstang's rankings give a rough but reliable view of how much attention literary magazines typically receive. There are separate lists for fiction, nonfiction, and poetry.

- **Erika Krouse's Ranking of 500 Literary Magazines for Short Fiction.** Erika Krouse's list can be used for any genre, even though its focus is short fiction. Instead of Garstang's Pushcart Prize–focused approach, Krouse uses a complex system based on prizes, circulation, payment to writers, and "coolness" to divide literary magazines into tiers. Her list includes information about each of these categories, plus deadlines, response time, and maximum word count. Her list is particularly helpful for thinking through which magazines are comparable to one another in terms of reputation.

Other rankings exist, if you want a different perspective. John Fox, at his blog *Bookfox*, assembles lists using criteria similar to Clifford Garstang's, except they are based on the *Best American Short Stories* anthology. Brecht De Poortere has assembled a database ranking lit mags based on their inclusion in an array of anthologies, as well as their number of X (formerly Twitter) followers. For science-fiction and fantasy writers, Eric Schwitzgebel runs a ranking of lit mags on his blog *The Splintered Mind.*

Small presses' prestige can be harder to track. This is in part because prestige is concentrated in books published by major, corporate publishers. Most major literary awards go to imprints owned by the Big 5, even if those imprints appear to be separate publishers. Prestige certainly exists in the small press world, but it's often based more on hearsay and reputation than on measurable recognition.

That said, several resources will give you an idea of which small presses are regularly receiving attention:

- **The CLMP Firecracker Awards.** The Firecracker Awards are given annually to small press books published in the categories of fiction, creative nonfiction, and poetry by the Community of Literary Magazines and Presses (CLMP), an organization that advocates for independent publishers. There are also awards for magazine/general excellence and magazine/best debut.
- **NEA grants.** Each year, the National Endowment for the Arts awards thousands of dollars to literary publishers. You can find the lists of awardees on the NEA's Recent Grants page, which will give you an idea of which publishers are deemed worthy of public support by the NEA panelists.
- **Book reviews.** Browsing book reviews will help you get a sense of which publishers' books are being read and considered publicly. Mainstream venues rarely pay attention to small press books, so make sure you find the right outlet. Review venues for small press literature include Full Stop, Rain Taxi, and The Rumpus. Many other literary magazines feature book reviews online or in print.
- **Additional literary awards.** Major awards like the Pulitzer and National Book Awards aren't great ways to rank small presses, since small presses aren't usually well represented (except in the poetry category). There are, however, awards that have proven more welcoming to small press writing, such as the Lambda Literary Awards and PEN Book Awards. Regional book awards, often organized by state, regularly make room for small presses as well.

All these lists come with your regularly scheduled caveat: rankings, honors, and awards only count as much as you let them. Let your own goals be a guide when deciding how important prestige is to you.

Unranked Lists

Instead of envisioning the literary world as a hierarchy of prestige, unranked lists represent each publication as part of a horizontally organized literary landscape. These lists don't claim to judge. The benefit of this approach is that it leaves the judging up to you.

The drawback of this approach, of course, is also that it leaves the judging up to you. How do you distinguish among so many publications? How do you know which is best, or best for you?

The most helpful unranked lists solve this problem by using tags and categories to narrow down publications based on criteria such as genre, word count, payment, submission fee, and deadlines. Here are the most reliable unranked lists:

- **Duotrope.** Duotrope is a long-standing comprehensive database with information on almost all active magazines and presses, including genre, style, word count, and payment, as well as submission response times. Built into Duotrope is a submissions tracker, if you prefer to use an external resource instead of your own system (see chapter 3). A full subscription to Duotrope costs $5 a month (as of this writing).
- **Chill Subs.** Chill Subs is like a free, Gen Z Duotrope (although some features have recently been monetized). Its database is large and ever-growing, and it takes a fun, irreverent approach to submissions.

Features include "Write or Die," which runs columns, interviews, and listicles; curated newsletters; and classes on writing and publishing.

- ***Writer's Market.*** *Writer's Market* is the well-known, regularly updated print guide to nearly every submission venue, including not only book publishers and literary magazines but also trade magazines, literary agencies, and contests and awards. Since it is published in a print edition, it can be particularly helpful for tactile readers who prefer to underline, dog-ear, and flip through pages.
- **Poets & Writers.** Poets & Writers, which is best known for its magazine about the craft and business of writing, maintains expansive databases of literary magazines, small presses, and literary contests and awards.
- **CLMP's directory of publishers.** The Community of Literary Magazines and Presses has a similarly extensive list of member presses and magazines.
- ***Heavy Feather Review.*** After *Entropy* shut its doors at the end of 2021, *Heavy Feather Review* took up the mantle of "Where to Submit," providing a regularly updated listing of small presses and journals that are open for submissions.

There are a number of other unranked listings, but they usually have few tags or categories, which makes them less easy to navigate. Among them are betweenthehighway press's publisher directory (which lists more than 1,500 presses) and *The Nonconformist*'s "Big, Big List of Indie Publishers and Small Presses." If you're looking to get a sense of the full breadth of small press publishing, these listings can act as a complement to the more robust resources listed above.

A final way to gain insight into the many publishers active

today is to browse the exhibitors at the major annual writing conference, Association of Writers & Writing Programs (AWP). These exhibitors are listed on AWP's website each year. Even better, if AWP (or another conference or book festival) happens to be taking place near you, you can attend and get to know the publications personally by visiting their exhibitor booths.

Getting Involved

The most long-term and, ultimately, most effective way to decide where to submit is to get involved in literary community. I know this is a lot to ask! It's hard enough just to find the time to write and submit. But getting involved doesn't have to be a major time suck. It includes all kinds of small actions you can sprinkle throughout your life. Once you take these steps, being an active part of the literary community often gives energy back to your writing — and to your life — in ways that more than justify the time and energy you put in.

The easiest way to get involved is simply by reading what small presses and literary magazines publish. There are many ways to find writing that inspires you:

- **Browse online literary magazines, subscribe to print literary magazines, and read books from a diversity of presses.** Reading literary magazines and writing published by small presses doesn't have to be a big financial investment, although it's good to support the publications you submit to. Libraries are often looking for new books to add to their collection, and by requesting books from small presses, you do both the presses and your local community a favor. If you want to become more familiar with the breadth of print magazines, many sell back copies (noncurrent issues) for as little as $5.

- **Attend local and online reading series.** Many communities have regular reading series, where a single author or a group of authors shares their work aloud and answers questions afterward. Readings take place at bookstores, bars, and coffee shops. In addition, the Zoom reading scene has taken off in the past few years. If you follow writers on social media, you're sure to see many announcements of online readings.
- **Use presses and magazines to guide your reading.** One of my favorite ways to read is by letting publication venues, rather than authors, guide my reading life. That is, if I like a book, instead of reading another book by that author, I'll read another book published by that press. This is a great way to recognize the thoughtful curatorial work editors put into selecting which writing to publish.
- **Research the publishing histories of authors you like.** If you discover a new author whose writing you like, look up which literary magazines and presses have published them in the past. Chances are, if you liked the author's work, the venues that have published their writing will appeal to you, too.

All the above are effective and long-lasting methods for getting familiar with the literary landscape. Remember how writing is like building a chair? "Sitting" in the product of someone's hard work is an active way of welcoming it into the world.

A more quantifiable, if more energy intensive, way of getting involved is to give your time and labor to a magazine or press. If you are particularly ambitious, you could start a press or a literary magazine of your own. But relatively few people have the time, inclination, skills, or funding to do that. Instead, I would suggest beginning with manageable contributions to one or two publications you feel particularly drawn to.

Here are some of the best ways to get started:

- **Write book reviews.** Nervous that you don't know how to write a book review? That's OK. Start by reading a few examples, then write about your experience of reading a book in the most generous and thoughtful way you can. Even if you are relatively inexperienced, the author and publisher will be grateful for your words. Reviews are a gift, both to small presses that don't receive mainstream media coverage and to the authors who publish with them.
- **Conduct interviews.** Like writing reviews, conducting interviews with authors allows you to be part of the conversation by engaging with others' work. Literary magazines are often looking for interviews to publish, and authors appreciate the chance to talk about their writing in a public forum.
- **Volunteer as a reader for a literary magazine.** Much of the initial work of evaluating submissions is done by readers who read everything that comes over the transom before recommending pieces to higher-up editors (see chapter 6). Literary magazines frequently need more readers to help them consider submissions more quickly. Some magazines will post calls for readers on their websites and social media.
- **Get involved in a reading series.** Bringing authors together for a regular literary reading is a great way to

meet people who are actively publishing books. Presses and writers always appreciate it when someone can host authors on tour. Consider offering to help with (or start) a reading series near you.

- **Participate in writing groups, workshops, and classes.** This option might not directly connect you with publishers, but it will help you build community with other writers. You can learn a lot from your writerly friendships, not only about writing and publishing but also about your own goals as a submitter. See appendix B for more suggestions on where to find literary community.

I believe in getting involved because it increases your familiarity with the literary landscape *and* helps you become an authentic part of it. When you're part of the conversation, deciding where to submit feels less like an attempt to break into an unfamiliar scene than a continual act of participation. Publication begins to fit into your life naturally. I can't promise that getting involved will help you get published, and you shouldn't think about your contributions as a quid pro quo. But you can treat your literary contributions as a gift to the community you're asking something from, too.

There is one final way to connect with writers, editors, and publishers: social media. Much of what I know about the literary landscape comes from years of X and Instagram, along with stints on Facebook. I know of no other way to keep up with so many interesting venues at once, to get a feel for their sensibilities, and to build a relationship with the work they are doing.

If you already have or choose to create a social media presence, think carefully about how you spend time on it. Which people, publishers, and communities do you want to be involved with? How can you use your time in the digital realm to end up with more inspiration, not less? How can social media act as a conduit to better reading, writing, and living rather than vacuuming all those things out of you?

Stay connected with your purpose in being on social media. Resist clickbait and distraction if you can. Go back for the new books you learn about, the new presses and magazines you come across, and the little interactions that make the literary world feel like it's filled with living, breathing people (it is!).

Regardless of which of the above strategies you prefer, getting involved is an essential tool for writers deciding where to submit. Seeing your work in print is most meaningful when you're part of a larger conversation — a conversation you're helping to grow.

If You're Submitting a Book

Submitting a full-length book or chapbook to a small press is an especially committed process. When you leap into book submissions, take the time to consider two additional factors.

Deepening Your Research

If you're submitting a full-length book, you've likely worked for years on it! Who you entrust with your writing is no small decision.

You can begin identifying presses by using the lists and the everyday practices discussed above. Soon, these practices will likely give way to more goal-directed, intentional research in the lead-up to submitting a book.

To strengthen your search for small presses to publish with, the following steps may be helpful:

- **From the library, check out several books published by each small press you are considering.** If they are not available through the main catalog, you can usually find small presses' books through interlibrary loan. Hold the books in your hand and ask yourself how you would feel if this was *your* book. Are the books high quality? Do you like their design? Do they fit your idea of what a book should look like?
- **Find out how their books are distributed.** Distribution determines whether readers can purchase books through bookstores and major online retailers. Some small presses sell only through their website or smaller distributors, which is helpful to know. Will your book be accessible where you want readers to find it?
- **Research other authors who publish with the press.** Do these authors have the outcomes *you* want as an author?
- **Check the publisher's presence on social media and elsewhere.** Will the press get the word out in a way that feels right to you? Will they build a strong website for your book? Do their books receive coverage in venues you appreciate?
- **Ask around.** Do you know anyone who has experience working with this press? Can you find interviews with the editors of the press? Learn as much as you can anecdotally, from unofficial sources as well as official ones.

Taking time to research small presses in depth before you submit to them will ensure that your publishing experience is as predictable as possible, even if there are bumps in the road, which there always are. The last thing you want is to publish a book with a press whose books you have never seen before. Your familiarity with the small presses where you submit will also allow you to tailor your cover letter, as discussed in chapter 5, so that you can let editors know why you believe your work is right for them.

A growing understanding of the small presses publishing today will also inspire your writing in unforeseen ways. Having a sense of the many editors and audiences who might read your work expands the possibilities of your writing. The more you read and research, the more your knowledge of your audience will appear on the page.

Large Small Presses and University Presses

When researching small presses, you may also encounter publications that have a different submission process than the one described in this book. Large small presses, which are independent in that they are not affiliated with the Big 5 houses, sometimes operate using the same publishing systems as the Big 5. These large small presses, also called midsize presses, might occasionally open submissions for special prizes that anyone can submit to. More often, however, they work with writers through literary agents. See appendix B for a list of books that can help you query agents.

University presses, too, are often mentioned in the same breath with small presses. Because they receive support from large, relatively stable institutions, university presses can take risks and support writing that commercial presses would not. But they also have widely varying, sometimes complicated submission processes, due in part to the fact that they publish scholarly works in addition to creative writing. Most university presses accept manuscripts from writers without agents. Some require only a cover letter, while others require a full book proposal. Many university presses also work with agented writers, especially as university presses' value in the literary world is increasingly acknowledged.

Even though university presses are not the focus of this book, much of my advice will apply to them. Their relationship to funding and to literary community is different from that of small presses, but it is worthwhile to consider university presses for your book. If you need to write a book proposal for your university press submission, *The Book Proposal Book* by Laura Portwood-Stacer is a helpful manual. For a guide to university presses that publish literary writing, take a look at the Association of University Presses Subject Area Grid, which lists university presses publishing fiction, creative nonfiction, poetry, and drama.

• • •

There you have it: a guide to finding every publication where you could possibly submit. Is it overwhelming? It kind of is. But these lists are only the beginning. As you research, you'll make your own lists of preferred venues for publication (see chapter 3) and narrow down your vision for what publication will look like.

If you're not sure where to begin, here's what I would do if I were just starting out. First, spend some time browsing the ranked lists. Do some journaling about your goals, think about what prestige means to you, and note the differences between more- and less-resourced venues for publication. When you're ready to submit, get a Duotrope account. I wouldn't keep the account forever, since it costs money, but I would use it for your first year or two of submitting in order to build your own criteria for submissions. Use Chill Subs and *Heavy Feather Review* to supplement, and the other lists when in doubt.

Once you've spent some time working through the above methods, consider how you might expand your involvement in literary community. You could change your reading habits to include one new literary magazine or a book published by a different small press each season. You could spend ten minutes each day searching for new publishers and authors to follow on social media. You could apply to be a reader for a lit mag. Take it slow and steady. Building literary community is a lifelong process.

Soon your relationship with submitting might take on a new life. When submitting your writing, you may no longer have to look up every literary magazine in the world. Instead of depending on ranked lists, you may carry a list of dream journals around in your head (or in a Google doc). You may know the exact search criteria to use on Duotrope or Chill Subs for each story, essay, or poem you write. While writing, you may even find yourself thinking, "This would be perfect for _____."

To me, this type of deeply interwoven relationship with publishing is the goal. Literary magazines and presses become not just places to publish your preexisting writing but active inspirations for your work. Your writing begins to feel like a conversation between you and every other writer and editor. Let publishers' work speak to you, and soon yours will speak to them, too.

• • •

Knowing about publication venues, however, is only part of deciding where to submit. The other part is knowing your writing itself. It's just as important to understand what you're bringing to the table as it is to understand what editors are looking for. A commitment to seeing your work through others' eyes will help you identify who might want to publish it.

There are several lenses through which you can understand your writing. Some are purely logistical, like word count. Others are contextual, like shared influences. Considering your writing through all these lenses gives you the best chance at finding a publication that will be receptive to your work.

Here are a few of the most important categories to consider when deciding where your writing might belong:

- **Word count.** Many publications have a minimum and maximum word count for submissions. If you are submitting a short story under a thousand words, for example, few magazines will consider it under their fiction category. You'd want to research venues that publish *flash* fiction instead. Another example: if you have a rather long poetry book, publishers may be less likely to consider it. Many presses draw the line at around eighty pages for poetry. Becoming familiar with the length standards of your genre may influence both your revision process and the publication venues you seek.
- **Genre.** Fiction, nonfiction, and poetry usually have separate editorial processes at magazines and presses, which means they also have three different categories for submission. My own writing often hovers at the edges of these categories or works between them, so I seek venues that accept hybrid or cross-genre work. You can also think about how a venue defines the genres they publish, which varies widely based on

taste. You can get a sense of what the editors think fiction, nonfiction, or poetry is by reading a few pages or excerpts.

- **Style.** Publications often prioritize either "traditional" or "experimental" styles, although this binary can be reductive. Have you written a personal essay with a clean narrative arc and an insight at the end? Try a publication with a more traditional aesthetic. Have you written a lyric essay full of disjunctive leaps between poetry, personal story, quotations, and all-caps homages to the moon? Try a more innovative publication. While both these essays are creative nonfiction, they'll likely find success at two fairly different kinds of publications. Understanding your own relationship to literary style will help you connect with those who have shared preferences.
- **Topic, subject, identity, or special interest.** Many literary magazines have special calls for writing on a theme or from a specific group of writers. These themes are usually broad enough to incorporate work that has already been written. Some journals have a theme for every issue; other publications are defined entirely by a single theme or focus. An important note: when you submit writing that matches a themed issue or a press's focus, be sure to mention it in the first paragraph of your cover letter.
- **Influences.** Which writers influence your writing? Which communities have informed your work? Locating where your writing comes *from* will influence where you send your writing *to*. For additional insight on where your writing might fit, seek the opinion of a fellow writer. We're often too close to our own writing

to fully understand its influences and echoes, and a trusted reader can help us identify them.

All this said, having a solid grasp of your writing isn't always about making sure your work fits an editor's taste. It's also essential to consider what your writing will *add* to the publication. Your writing stands to transform the venues that publish it. That's why publishing is a conversation — it's where the needs of an editor and the vision of an author meet.

Don't let the above categories limit your writing. If your writing doesn't conform to any of these categories, great! If it falls neatly into them but does something beautiful with the form, great, too! You don't need to fit inside a box or go out of your way to break one. The key is to develop a relationship with the box that an editor has never seen before.

• • •

Finally, I want to remind you to stay connected to your goals when deciding where to submit. It's particularly important to consider time frame, audience, and your intuition when deciding how the submission venues you choose match up with your goals.

When considering time frame, ask yourself the following questions: How quickly do you want to receive a response to your submission? How quickly do you want it to be published if it is accepted? How timely is the subject matter of what you've written?

In general, larger, more prestigious venues take longer to get back to you. Waiting six months to a year is the norm. After you receive an acceptance from this type of publication, it could take more than a year to see your writing in print. Smaller, less prestigious venues, on the other hand, receive fewer submissions. Usually (but not always) they get back to you more quickly and publish sooner than the bigger venues.

Receiving an acceptance on the sooner side can be a welcome source of immediate feedback on your work. Waiting for years can make your writing feel like ancient history by the time it is published. Then again, if you have the patience, receiving an acceptance at a well-known venue can be worth the wait. The calculation here, like so many of the calculations involved in submitting, depends on your goals: how quickly you want to see your writing published or how long you are willing to wait.

A second consideration related to your goals is who you want to communicate with. If your goal is to make your story as widely accessible as possible, you might choose an online literary magazine or a press that publishes in ebook as well as in print format. If your goal is to share your story with a specific readership, you might match the work with a venue that is focused on reaching that readership. If you are excited by the idea of seeing your work on the shelves of your local bookstore, you might submit to the literary magazines your bookstore carries and the independent presses whose books they stock.

The last consideration, but by no means a less vital one, is your intuition. Your imagination, your senses, your gut feeling: all these play an essential role in how good you'll feel about a magazine or press publishing your work.

In the interest of honoring that intuition, pause for a minute before you make a final decision about where to submit your work. Envision the poem, essay, story, or book you're sending out. What will it look like when it's published? Which publication *feels* right? Are you authentically excited about a particular literary magazine or press? Do you just *know* who will publish it, with a deep sense of where the work belongs?

Listen to this feeling. The magazine or press you connect with may not always be the most prestigious or logistically sensible one. But prestige and logistics don't have to be the final measure of your writing.

Each piece of writing is its own moment, a leap into being newly in the world. Believe in the bridges you can build with your writing. Imagine where those bridges could lead.

3

Getting Set Up

Once you figure out why to submit and where, you're almost ready to send out your writing. All that remains is getting organized, which includes creating the files you'll use to keep track of submissions, developing documents that streamline your efforts, and placing everything in an accessible location. It won't take long to bring the necessary materials together, and you will thank yourself later when they've grown into detailed accounts of your submission experiences.

There are several good reasons for investing time in developing these files at the outset. Practically speaking, staying organized is essential to making your process more efficient, effective, and respectful. It will allow you to see the status of your submissions at any time, which will inform how you continue to approach each submission. Where is a piece currently under consideration? How many publications have responded, and how many are you waiting on? Having easy-to-find answers to these questions allows you to make decisions about when to submit, when to wait, and when to return to the drawing board. This setup also makes it easy to do an essential task that is requested by almost all editors: withdrawing your work from other publications once you receive an acceptance.

The benefit of having an organized set of materials goes

beyond logistics. It also encourages you to compartmentalize your submissions process, locating it in a physical place on your computer that you can return to when it's time to submit. The rest of the time, you can focus on the writing itself — and on living in the real world — knowing the many threads of your submissions are well accounted for.

Your Essential Documents

The documents I recommend are drawn from my own experience of keeping track of submissions. But everyone's setup will be different. As you send out your work and determine what kind of information matters to you, you'll likely change the style and organization of your documents. That's good! Let your experience shape your process.

Additionally, your documents do not need to be devoted exclusively to nose-to-the-grindstone work. Let them be places of refuge, reflection, and imagination. In my submissions document, for example, I sometimes write a celebratory note to myself after an acceptance, including emojis, exclamation points, and reflections on getting the news. After a vexing rejection, I may add a note encouraging myself to stay with a piece I really believe in. My file becomes a kind of journal in those moments, where I can say what I feel about the process. You can keep track, be detail oriented, and still stay in touch with the emotional side of the submissions process.

Keeping Track of Active Submissions

Your first document is the bread and butter of your submission materials. Its job is to keep track of every submission you've ever sent, as well as the response to that submission.

At the very least, your entries for each submission should include the following:

- **Title.** Which piece of writing you submitted.
- **Venue.** The literary magazine or small press where you submitted.
- **Date of submission.** Sometimes I include expected response time alongside this, if the publication makes it available in their submission guidelines.
- **Response.** Acceptance? Rejection? Encouraging rejection? Include the date you received the response so you can refer to it later when estimating the realistic response time for that publication.

You can organize this information in several different ways, based on your formatting preferences and the software you use. I use a simple text-based Google document where I can control formatting and add notes here and there. My document has a heading for each piece I send out, and below it a line for each time I submit the piece. Each line includes title, venue, date of submission, response, and date of response. If a piece is still out on submission, I leave the text black. I change it to red if I receive a rejection. I use orange for a positive rejection, and, if the sun is shining on me and I receive an acceptance, I change the line to green and make the text bold for good measure.

Many writers use Excel or Google spreadsheets. You can find a preformatted, fillable spreadsheet on writer Matt Bell's website. Other writers use a submissions tracking system that's integrated with a larger online database, such as Duotrope. Using Duotrope's submission tracker keeps their tools at your fingertips and integrates your data with their information about response time.

However you choose to keep track of submissions, create a system and stick to it. Plan for a system that will work even when you submit many, many pieces of writing. After a few years of sending out your work, you will have quite a lot to keep track of. Again, you'll thank yourself if you build an easy, organized system now.

Aspirations and Possibilities

A second document, which lists aspirations and possibilities for your submissions, allows you to preserve your personal archive of knowledge about submitting. It might feel auxiliary at first, and I admit that I hadn't realized I needed such a file when starting out. But after several years of sending out my writing, I realized I was reinventing the wheel every time I sent out a submission.

The below lists allow you to preserve the results of your research, which will grow into a stable launching pad for all your submissions. With their help, you can become your own authoritative resource for your submissions goals. There are a few valuable sections to include. I keep these lists in the same file, but you can separate them if that works better for you.

Literary Mags and Presses Where You Want to Be Published

After becoming familiar with the resources listed in chapter 2, you will soon develop a personalized sense of your dream magazines and presses for publication. These dream venues will reflect your priorities as a writer, which means they will differ from the strictly prestige-based lists.

There are many ways to organize your list of publications to submit to, but one great example is Erika Krouse's list (see chapter 2). Instead of ranking venues, she organizes them into tiers. Creating your own tiered lists of preferred submission venues allows you to structure your submissions in easily navigable sets, sending out to five to eight venues at a time without having to parse the desirability of each one for each submission.

Deadlines and Reading Periods

Publication venues aren't always open exactly when you want them to be. Sometimes their reading period is months away, and you need a reminder to return when submissions are open. Other times, a deadline is coming up soon and you want to keep revising until the last possible second. Keeping an organized, chronological list of deadlines will help you focus on the right submissions at the right time for your writing.

Return to this file regularly. Consider setting aside a specific time each month to check on upcoming deadlines, reviewing whether any submission periods have opened recently. You can also place reminders on your daily calendar.

Literary Magazines and Presses That Have Sent Positive Rejections

Always keep a list of the publications that have sent you encouraging rejections. You will record positive responses in your main submissions document as well, but it helps to have a dedicated spot where you can see every venue that has encouraged your writing. I organize my list chronologically, so every time I get a positive rejection from a venue, that venue moves to the top of the list.

Another related list you can keep includes publications

where you know someone or feel particularly welcome to submit. Knowing an editor won't necessarily mean receiving an acceptance, but, as with submitting after a positive rejection, it can increase the chance that your submission will be read closely.

General Notes about Your Submission Strategy

As you hone your submission strategy (the subject of chapter 4), it can be helpful to take account of that strategy on a regular basis. Think of this document like a submitting diary, charting your progress, goals, and feelings about sending out your writing. Having a concrete timeline can help ground these reflections. Questions include: What are your goals for the next six months of submitting? What actions will you take to achieve those goals? How are you feeling about submitting? What can you do to bring life to the process?

These self-check-ins help ground your submitting practice, keeping you connected to your overall plan so you don't feel at sea every time you jump into submitting again.

Cover Letter Template

The third document you'll need contains materials for your cover letter, which is important enough that I devote a whole chapter of this book to it (chapter 5). The cover letter is your one chance to communicate directly to editors, framing the writing you've submitted and contextualizing yourself as a writer.

But you don't need to compose your cover letter anew each time you submit. Instead, you can rely on a boilerplate letter that you tailor to each submission. This will streamline the process of sending out your work, buying you more time for the personalization we'll talk about in chapter 5.

Why It's So Important to Keep Track of Positive Rejections

I've mentioned positive rejections a lot in this chapter. But what *are* positive rejections? Why keep track of them? How do you know when you've received one? What do they mean?

Positive rejections result from the fact that most publications have a tiered system of responding to submissions. Editors choose from three types of letters to send in response to submitting writers: An acceptance offers publication. A standard rejection turns the writing down politely, without specific encouragement. A positive rejection is still a rejection, but it includes words of encouragement on your specific submission. It means you came close to publication but didn't make it this time.

Positive rejections are often as short as standard rejections. They typically do two things: First, they say the editors took a particular interest in your writing, considered it closely, enjoyed reading it, or had a conversation about publishing it. Second, they close with an invitation or encouragement to submit more writing to their publication.

If a letter includes these two things — praise and an invitation to submit again — you can be fairly sure it is a positive rejection. This means the editors took an active interest in your work and would be gratified to see more of your writing in their queue.

Sometimes these letters can be confusing. If a letter thanks you for the privilege of considering your work and encourages future submissions, do they mean *your* work in particular, or are they just being polite and trying to drum up future submissions in general? If they say they enjoyed your work but don't invite you to submit again, is this just the letter they are sending to everybody?

Reading these letters can feel like trying to decipher a code you don't have the key for. In fact, an entire website, called Rejection Wiki, is devoted to crowdsourcing different publications' rejection letters for just this reason. Comparing notes on Rejection Wiki allows writers to figure out what tier of rejection they received so that they can determine whether their writing was received positively.

There is one type of positive rejection you won't have to speculate about. This is a personal rejection, in which an editor addresses specific aspects of your piece rather than (or in addition to) a form response. This kind of letter indicates that an editor has taken the time to read your work closely *and* to offer feedback on it. Often this feedback takes the form of praise and, if you're lucky, it might also include feedback about improvements you can make to the piece. I take these personalized rejections seriously. They are a sign that the editor cares about your work and wants to see it reach its final form.

Personal or not, positive rejections are important because they build a relationship between you and an editor, magazine, or press. You're no longer the only party interested in seeing your writing published with them — now they're interested in publishing you as well. Remember that most editors do the work they do because they want to find new and compelling writing. When you get a positive response, even if it declines your work, it's a sign that editors are rooting for you, hoping your next piece will be right for them.

Writing Prompt

Your submission materials will become a virtual home for your practice of working toward publication. But what about a physical home? Use this prompt to imagine a place that supports your submission practice.

With your eyes closed, envision yourself sitting down to work on submissions. Picture your ideal place for this work. Think of an inspiring, energy-giving space where you have everything you need at your fingertips. Notice the details that will help you have a successful session of submitting your writing, including the time of day.

Where are you sitting? How is your space organized? Do you have a cup of tea next to you? Imagine taking a breath and settling in. Now begin to write about this place.

As you write, reflect on how you can work toward creating such a space in real life. What concrete steps can you take? Some examples: Organize your desk. Write down your submitting goals and tack them to a bulletin board. Carve out a time in your busy schedule for this important work.

Formatting

Now that you've got your files set up, you need to make sure you're presenting your manuscript properly. Boring is better when it comes to formatting. You want your page layout to be unremarkable, standard, and totally ordinary.

Standard formatting allows editors to focus on the content of your work. When reading hundreds of submissions, editors prefer when the differences in the writing itself (rather than the format) stand out. A burst of color or a fun font may grab an editor's attention, but not in a way that makes them appreciate the work. Instead, it suggests a lack of familiarity with the submission process. Sticking to standard formatting conveys to readers and editors that you are taking your writing seriously and know the professional standards.

The guidelines below give you the format most publications will ask you to follow. Some publications' guidelines will differ from the below; always prioritize the guidelines of the venue where you are submitting.

Standard manuscript format looks like the following:

Font: Times New Roman. Some writers use Garamond or other fancier-looking typefaces. This is unnecessary.

Size: 12 point. Don't overthink this one.

Margins: 1 inch on every side.

Spacing: Double-spaced for prose, single-spaced for poetry. Between sentences, include only *one* space. If you include two, editors will just have to take the extra space out.

Information about the author: Include your name, address, phone number, and email address on the top left of a submission's first page. This should be single-spaced. Note that a few submissions venues — including most contests — ask for anonymous submissions without your name or identifying information on the manuscript or even in the file name. If this is the case, make sure you do *not* have your name or personal information in the document.

Word count: Include the approximate word count of the piece one line below the information about the author. Some people include this at the top right of the first page instead. Round the word count to the next 500 words, or to the next 1,000 words for book manuscripts. A word count is usually not needed for poetry.

Title: Centered, with no additional formatting (no need to use bold or italics), above the first line of the piece. Poetry may need formatted titles, since it includes more titles and a less clear distinction between title and poem.

Beginning of a paragraph: Indent half an inch. Use the ruler at the top of the page to indent the first lines of paragraphs rather than using spaces or the tab key (this makes layout easier for page designers once it is accepted). Don't add extra lines between paragraphs unless you are using them to indicate a section break.

Section breaks: You have a little leeway in how to express section breaks, also known as scene breaks, which come between scenes in a short story or sections in an essay. The pound sign (#), centered, is standard for typesetters. An asterisk also works. Some writers just skip one or two lines between sections, but this can get confusing if a page break arrives at the same place as a section break. There is no need to get more creative than this. Your piece may ultimately be laid out with an interesting signature symbol between the sections, but you do not need to include symbols like these in the manuscript (except in rare cases when it is essential to the writing). If you are submitting poetry, every poem should begin on a new page.

Page numbers: Include page numbers in the bottom right corner of the document, unless the venue asks for a different positioning.

Remember, this format is not an official standard sent down from the mountaintop. It is a set of general conventions that change over time.

Formatting also changes with experimentation as the work requires it. Cross-genre and hybrid writing is prone to this sort of innovation, and poetry permits it as well. When deciding whether to follow standard formatting, the question to consider is, Would the writing work just as well if it was standardly formatted? If the answer is yes, stick with the standard format. If the answer is no — if something would be lost by using the standard format — diverge as much as the writing requires.

Finally, remember that the name of your document can usually be seen by editors. Many of us work in documents with names like "Weird cat story_final FINAL2.2 (THIS IS REALLY THE FINISHED ONE!!!)," and we may not want to share that with those who are reading our writing for the first time. Cleaning up the file name is another small but significant gesture that allows your writing to be seen in the best light. Use the title of your story or essay, or "Five Poems" if you are submitting poems, then a dash or parentheses and your last name.

Money

Money matters when it comes to submitting your writing. How much will submitting cost you? How much will publishing earn you? Is it realistic to expect to make money from publishing your writing, given the costs of submitting?

Before delving into the details, it's helpful to recognize that writing often comes from a place that has little to do with our finances. For many of us, writing arises from a deep desire to communicate — a need to make something happen in the world with language. Even when we buy books, a more important exchange is happening than the exchange of dollars. We attach the necessity of money to writing later on.

I believe the same goes for editors, who are far from well paid, especially those who work for small presses and literary magazines. The small press world is full of people reading manuscripts, building websites, and hand-assembling chapbooks in their basements or garages, working in pairs or in threes to sustain publications that look much bigger from the outside. They publish writing and work with writers because they believe in it, and when it comes to finances, they are, like us, just doing their best to survive.

So how do we deal with money, then? How do we survive when we practice an art form that isn't staked primarily on financial exchange?

One possible answer is to forget about the financial aspects of publishing, earning your money elsewhere and treating your writing as a separate pursuit. This approach frees you to write exactly what you want, when you want. If you can make it work, by all means focus on your writing to the exclusion of financial concerns. For many writers, the separation between work and writing is a generative one. For others, this separation can be difficult, especially if we are working jobs that leave us little free time. This is why some writers choose to intertwine their careers and their writing: when we put a little economic pressure on our writing, we are more likely to center it in our lives.

A second approach, therefore, is to focus your submissions (and your writing itself) toward building a financially sustainable career. By pursuing publication, you build a portfolio of writing that allows you to get teaching jobs, speaking engagements, article assignments from paying publications, and even ghostwriting gigs. Others focus their energy on building their reputation as freelance editors, touting their own publications as proof that they can help edit a writer's manuscript toward publication. Even the most successful writers of fiction, creative nonfiction, and poetry rarely live off writing alone. But it is possible to cobble together writing-related jobs that add up to a reasonable salary.

The reality is that most of us follow some combination of these two approaches. We may come to writing for freedom, inspiration, and its distance from everyday concerns. We may love it because it is *not* a commodity. At the same time, the pressures of survival affect what we do with our writing. Earning money is not the point, but we do need to earn money. So we make the thing we love work for us.

How do you balance these priorities? How do you write on your own terms while earning enough to live on? It is important to acknowledge that your approach is not simply a matter of personal choice. We make decisions about our writing based on our incomes, our savings, our class status, the support we receive from our families, and the overall precarity or stability of our financial situation.

Small presses and literary magazines play a special role in the financial side of writing. Small presses don't usually pay as much as Big 5 houses, and literary magazines rarely pay more than a small honorarium. What small presses and lit mags *do*, uniquely, is publish writing that may not be considered marketable or guaranteed to sell a lot of copies. Writers can use these publications to build a financially sustainable life.

In my case, publishing with small presses and literary magazines has enabled me to get paid for writing-adjacent work. After publishing widely and earning an MFA and a PhD, I lucked into a job at a well-paying college with a reasonable teaching load. While I don't get paid to write, exactly, my teaching load is limited enough that I can spend an hour or two a day on my creative writing. My job also provides external motivation to write, since I regularly present myself to students and colleagues as a creative writer.

There are many ways to approach the financial side of writing. You may rely more on teaching writing than on selling the actual work. You may have a strong career outside of writing, which frees you to be more flexible about the money you make from publications. Or you may aim to live off your writing. In this case, you will focus on submissions that build your case for paid opportunities in the future. You can then slowly transition to writing exclusively for payment over the next few years.

These options, and so many others, only make sense if they make sense for *you*. It is your prerogative to decide how money intersects with your writing, given your financial situation and goals for the future.

The Cost of Submissions

Many of us hope to receive money for our writing. The reality, however, is that first you will likely have to pay to submit your writing.

Before electronic submissions, this wasn't the case. Most literary magazines and small publishers took submissions through the mail. Writers paid only for paper, envelopes, and postage. This process was slow. For the writer, it took time, effort, and organization, which limited the number of people who submitted. A physical rejection slip was the response to declined submissions: a piece of paper that came back to you in a self-addressed stamped envelope (SASE) in the mail.

Only a small number of publications use this process today. The overwhelming majority take submissions online, enabling them to read submissions faster and make submitting more accessible. The downside of this convenience, however, is that online submission manager software costs money. By now, Submittable is the submission manager of choice for most mags and presses. Submission venues are responsible for its costs, rather than writers paying the cost of postage, as in the past.

Opinions differ on who ultimately should cover these costs. Some editors are vehement that writers shouldn't have to pay to submit their writing. These editors foot the bill for Submittable themselves or set up another low-cost option (like email or the old free Submission Manager). Other publications pass these costs on to the writer, charging $3 to $5 for a literary magazine submission and $20 to $40 for a book submission. When charged across hundreds of submissions, these fees often amount to more than Submittable's cost. Many presses channel the additional income toward the costs of publishing their books, paying for their website, and even paying writers, a model in which money passes from the hands of many submitting writers into the hands of the few who are selected for publication.

There are two sides to the issue of submission fees. On

the one hand, charging submission fees limits submissions to writers who have easy access to funds. Submitting is expensive, especially because you usually have to submit to multiple publications before you receive an acceptance. Some publications offer a fee waiver for this reason, asking for payment from those who can pay and waiving it for those who cannot. Some publications promise they will never charge submission fees.

On the other hand, expecting publishers to cover submission fees limits who can start a literary magazine or press. If you need a lot of money to start a publishing outfit, the future of literature remains in the hands of people with expendable wealth. Publishers who charge for submissions typically aren't getting rich off submission fees. They are doing so to keep their operations above water.

So it's a hard question, and one I recommend approaching with generosity toward both writers and editors. Everyone wants to be compensated fairly for their work, and no one wants to pay to be a writer or editor.

Personally, I pay to submit my writing. Submission fees are a widespread reality, and I am lucky to have the funds to cover my submissions. The costs have added up over the years, but I've slowly made them back through the money I've earned from publishing. Plus, I have had the opportunity to submit much more widely than I would without paying submission fees. At the end of the day, paying the fees has been worth it.

Let's Talk Numbers

So what is submitting actually going to cost you? I'll share a few numbers, but only as examples. Experiences vary widely based on where you choose to submit and how many times you submit before receiving an acceptance.

Here's one example. Let's say you have to submit to ten literary magazines to receive an acceptance. If half those magazines charge for submissions, and each costs $3, you would spend $15 sending out one story, essay, or set of poems. This would be a favorable acceptance rate, so I would estimate a higher cost per submitted piece than this.

What if you're sending out a book? Let's say you need to send it to twenty venues in order to receive an acceptance, a very favorable acceptance rate for a book, and half of them charge for submissions. These submissions cost up to $40, perhaps $30 on average. Ten submissions at $30 each is $300 — and that's if the book gets picked up quickly. In submitting a book widely, especially if you are submitting to presses that use the contest model, you will likely end up paying several hundred dollars.

If you choose to submit to magazines or presses that don't charge for submissions, of course, your submissions will always be free. Many venues, especially presses, take pride in maintaining free submissions. On the other hand, if you submit to contests, your submission costs will add up more quickly.

Should I Submit to Contests?

Contests are the most expensive way to submit your writing. Many literary magazines that charge a $3 submission fee also run contests that have a $20 to $30 entry fee. These contests usually feature a well-known judge who picks the winner, as well as a prize of around $1,000. Sometimes they promise publication for the finalists as well as the winner, who is always published. It's tempting to submit to impressive-sounding contests. Winning feels like a worthy form of validation for your writing.

But *is* it worth it? If your goal is solely to publish your writing, literary magazine contests are not the most efficient path. Your money can get you much farther if you submit during a magazine's regular reading period, where the submission fee is a fraction of the contest fee. Also, regular submissions are usually open more frequently than contests.

If you are looking for a prestigious-sounding qualification next to your name, literary magazine contests are one place to earn this kind of qualification. Just know that these contests can be competitive, especially at prestigious journals.

Book and chapbook contests are, however, a valuable option for any writer submitting a book, and I would recommend submitting to them in order to give you the highest chance of publication. Many presses accept full-length submissions only through contests. Book contests are often run similarly to literary magazine contests, with a guest judge, prize money, and the promise of publication for the winner. The difference is the outcome: a prizewinning, full-length book you wrote published by a reputable small press.

This outcome will have a much bigger effect on your writing life than a literary magazine publication with a prize attached to it. Having a book to your name qualifies you for jobs and speaking opportunities, not to mention the very real sense of accomplishment that comes with publishing a book.

A Word on Self-Publishing

Self-publishing is another way to put money toward publication, but it is different from paying submission fees. If a press asks you to pay them to publish your writing — or if it requires you to guarantee a certain number of purchases of your work — they are a vanity publisher, and working with them is self-publishing. Hybrid publishing is a related publishing method, in which authors share expenses with the publisher.

Self-publishing is a legitimate way to share your writing with the world, but it is different from publishing with small presses and literary magazines.

There's a difference, first of all, in the publisher's investment in you as an author. If you are publishing with a vanity press, they make money when you pay them to print the book. They therefore have little motivation to promote your book, since they've already recouped their costs by printing it. They get their money from you, not from moving copies.

People and institutions may view your writing differently, too, if it is self-published rather than published with a selective press. Big 5 and small press books are vetted, as is the writing published in most literary magazines. It's not necessarily valid to judge the quality of writing based on how it has been published, but it is true that self-publishing generally does not involve a selection process.

Most importantly, self-publishing does not come with a built-in audience or following. This is why self-publishing works best for those who already know their audience and are connected to them directly. For those who don't, it can be difficult to get the book into the hands of readers who are not family members and close friends.

Publishing with a small press, on the other hand, links you to a whole new community. This community includes the editors who select your writing, the writers publishing with the same press or magazine, and the community of readers the publisher is connected with. These connections are always expanding, which is why publishing with a small press or literary magazine can set off a chain reaction of community building for authors.

Making Money from Your Writing

What about getting paid? As discussed above, small presses and literary magazines are often driven by priorities other than financial reward. Even Big 5 houses rarely pay enough to allow writers to live off their writing. This leaves most writers dependent on a separate job, a partner, family support, or another form of income.

Your writing can nonetheless supplement your income and make a difference in your life, depending on your expenses and situation. Below I'll discuss a rough range of possibilities so you know what to expect when it comes to payment.

Let's Talk Numbers

Payment for publication in literary magazines and journals is almost always nominal. For many small literary magazines, payment is nothing at all, given that they are run by one or two people funding the work out of their own pockets and working on the magazine for free. Slightly more money is available from established or institutionally affiliated literary magazines, often in the vein of $25 to $50. It's only in the most prestigious fifty or so literary magazines that the numbers increase precipitously, sometimes landing between $20 and $50 per page, though many have a flat fee of around $100, and some just pay two contributor copies and a year's subscription. Erika Krouse's lit mag rankings (see chapter 2) are a helpful tool for getting a sense of each literary magazine's pay rates.

Payment is higher for full-length books, although what you get paid almost never recoups the time and energy you've put into the writing. Many presses operating on the contest model offer a prize of $1,000 to $2,000, plus royalties and twenty to fifty copies of your book. Those not operating on a contest model tend to be less clear about their terms on their submission pages, waiting until acceptance to inform you about compensation. The most prestigious small presses offer payment in the thousands. Several hundred dollars is more common. Others offer only royalties. Very small presses — micropresses that publish chapbooks, for instance — might print a hundred hand-stitched or stapled copies and give you twenty as payment.

Very occasionally, you will hear of a publisher who did not follow through on their financial commitment to writers. This usually accompanies the public implosion of a small press or the exposure of a literary magazine's unfair publishing practices. These moments serve as a helpful warning to those of us submitting our writing. Most publications are doing their best, but even good intentions can fall flat without a commitment to transparency toward writers, especially when it comes to payment.

Reliable publications regularly prove, by the quality of the books they release and the testimony of writers they publish, that they prioritize writers and pay them as much as possible while keeping their publication sustainable. This is another reason why community matters: shared involvement in literary publications creates accountability and information sharing that can inform your decisions about who to publish with.

Enter a publishing relationship with a critical eye, but follow through on that relationship with a sense of trust. If a publication can't pay you as much as you wish, they are likely not making money off your work either. You are in this together.

Finishing Your Manuscript

There's one last thing you need to prepare for submitting, which is also the first thing: the writing itself. Is your piece truly ready for the editorial process? Have you put your heart into it, not just in the drafting process but in repeated revisions?

Pouring yourself into the writing is *the* best way to prepare for submitting. Feeling confident about your work gives you solid ground to stand on amid a submission process fraught with ups, downs, and long waits. The writing itself is always at the center of editors' experience of a submission, and it should be at the heart of yours, too.

Whether you receive a rejection or an acceptance, whether you wait a week or a year for a response, remember that your writing is unique and essential. You don't need anyone else to tell you that. Your writing resonates all on its own.

4

Your Strategy

Once you have your materials organized, it's time to make a plan. Yes, you heard me: a plan. While it may be tempting to fling your writing out to the very first publications you find, you will have a more fulfilling experience of submitting by thinking through your strategy beforehand.

The word *strategy* is loaded. It can feel warlike or, at the very least, disingenuous. You don't want to treat your writing like a battle. But strategy doesn't have to live apart from community and connection. Being strategic simply means identifying your goals and working toward them.

You can be strategic, in other words, while respecting the editors you submit to. That's because your interests and the editors' align. You want to find the person who sees your writing for its unique magic. Editors want to find writing that clicks with their sensibility. The goal of your submission strategy is to allow this connection to arise.

Strategies for All of Us

You'll likely navigate all the below questions as you build your submission strategy. Understanding the rough shape of these questions will allow you to make decisions based on your stated goals.

Tiered Submissions

Deciding how many venues to submit to at a time, as well as which venues to submit to, is a constant negotiation. You have to consider a number of questions: How selective is each publication? What is each publication's response time? Should I wait for my favorite publication to get back to me before I submit to those I'm less interested in? How can I make sure my writing gets published in a reasonable amount of time?

It's exhausting and, for most of us, unsustainable, to agonize over these questions every time we submit. This is why the logic of tiers reigns for many submitters. Relying on tiers to guide your submissions saves you from rebuilding your submission list for every piece you send. Using tiers also ensures that you don't receive an acceptance from a less desirable venue when a more desirable one is still considering your writing.

With tiered submissions, you submit in small groups of publications based on your preference for those publications. Your first tier includes publications where you would most like to be published. If the first tier doesn't work out, you submit to the next tier, which has slightly less preferable publications. If that doesn't work out, you submit to the next tier, and so on. The only calculation involved, once you've chosen your tiers, is when to send out the next round of submissions.

Here's an example. You've just finished a short story, and you're ready to send it out. With the tiering system, you submit to your top five literary magazines at once. You may have slight preferences among these literary magazines. But the idea is that you would be equally happy if any of them accepted it, and so you're giving them all an equal chance at the story. This group of magazines is your first tier.

Over the next few months, four of the journals get back to you with rejections. No problem. You planned for this. Even though there's still one first-tier publication looking at the story, it's time to send out to the next tier. This tier is a little bigger: maybe it includes seven literary magazines. This tier is also less competitive, so you have a better chance at receiving an acceptance. Even if you're slightly less excited about this tier of literary magazines, you'd still feel great if one of them accepted the story.

Maybe you get an acceptance during this round. If so, great! If most of the journals respond in the negative, submit to your next tier. Keep working down the list until you've exhausted the publications you'd be interested in publishing with.

Grouping submissions in this way takes the pressure off. You don't have to constantly think about submissions, reevaluating your strategy with every new development. You just have to submit to the next tier when you've heard back from the previous one.

The main variables to manage are how to construct your tiers and when to send out the next round of submissions. Additionally, you may want to adjust your tiers for each piece of writing based on genre, style, and audience.

How to Construct Your Tiers

We'll talk later in this chapter about how to choose a publication that matches your goals. But you also need to decide how *many* magazines or presses to submit to in one go. How many publications you submit to comes down to how long you're willing to wait. The fewer places you submit to, the more selective you can be about who publishes your writing and the longer your wait for acceptance will be. The more places you submit to, the more likely you'll get an acceptance quickly. Submitting too selectively can mean waiting years for an acceptance. A middle ground is to submit to five to eight literary magazines or presses at a time.

When to Send Out the Next Tier of Submissions

Response times are ever-fluctuating, even with a single publication, meaning you can never be certain when you will receive a response. Some literary magazines get back to you as quickly as two weeks. Others take as long as a year and a half. Long response times are the norm. Since waiting for *every single venue* to get back to you could take over a year, it often makes sense to send out your next tier before every venue in the previous tier has responded.

This means that your tiers blur into one another over time. If I've heard back from three of five magazines in my first tier after six months, for example, I would send out to my second tier in order to ensure that the piece still has a chance of being published in the next year. Once I've run through several tiers, I might even stop tiering my submissions, instead submitting to one or two new magazines for every magazine that rejects me. At this stage, I try to have each piece out at four or five venues at any one time.

Tiering gets more complicated when it comes to book submissions. Many presses open sporadically, or only once a year, and most take at least nine months to respond to submissions. This means you can really only submit your book to one tier of submissions a year. If you are too picky, you might wait years to receive an acceptance.

This is where you have to be realistic with your goals. Which is more important to you, limiting submissions to a few select presses or seeing your book published soon? If you want your book to be published in the next few years, you may have to be less particular about where you submit. A middle way would be to take one year to be incredibly selective about your submissions, take a second year to be a little selective, and take a third year to not be selective at all. That would put you on three yearlong tiers for your submissions.

The wait times are long, I know. Publishing, like writing, happens slowly. Remember that being published in your dream literary magazine or press often takes a number of tries. Achieving your publishing goals is the work of many manuscripts, many years, and many submissions.

Simultaneous Submissions

Most publications understand that writers submit to several venues at the same time, and they accept simultaneous submissions with the understanding that writers will withdraw their piece immediately if it is accepted somewhere else. Do note, however, that a few literary magazines and small presses ask submitters for an exclusive look at their writing, which can throw a stick in the spokes of a tiered submission process.

I typically steer clear of publications that do not allow simultaneous submissions, unless I believe a piece I have written is perfect for that venue and that venue only. The realities of submitting — especially the wait times discussed above — make exclusive submissions an inefficient way to achieve your publication goals.

One exception to this is solicited submissions. If an editor asks you directly to submit your piece to their publication, it is reasonable (and in most cases, the right thing to do) to wait until you have heard back from them to submit to other venues.

If Your Work Is Declined

Another good thing about tiering submissions is you have a built-in plan in case of rejection: simply go to the next tier and send out more submissions. This plan takes away the necessity of reevaluating your submission at every stage of the process. Rejection is a normal part of submitting your writing. You will receive far more rejections than you receive acceptances, even if you are a successful writer. Just stay with the process.

That said, rejections do have *some* meaning. Five rejection letters are to be expected. Ten rejection letters are the norm. Fifteen rejection letters on a short piece of writing shouldn't scare you, but at this point you might want to start thinking about your relationship to your story, essay, or poem and how you want it to live in the world. After you receive twenty or twenty-five rejections, it can be helpful to have a plan for reassessing or rewriting the piece.

Not all rejections are equal. If your rejection letters are peppered with encouraging notes, consider it a sign that editors like your writing but that it just hasn't clicked perfectly yet. Don't be shy when continuing to send out a piece that has gotten a good number of positive rejections. It might need a rewrite or a few more rounds of judicious revision, but something there has editors excited about your work.

If you're getting a lot of rejections without any encouraging notes, it might be time to kick your contingency plan into gear. Ask yourself: How much do I believe in this piece of writing? Is it worth it to keep going back to it over and over, revising, resubmitting, and playing the waiting game? If it *is* worth it — if you really believe in the piece — stay with it as long as you can. But if you prefer to work on something else, if you feel comfortable letting that piece go, *do* let it go. Tabling a manuscript can feel like failure. Think of it instead as a kind of success. Moving on gives you a chance to reprioritize. Choose the writing that matters most to you. Focus on the work you can't let go of.

When you're submitting a book, you should expect even more rejections. Many writers reach as many as sixty or seventy rejections and still ultimately publish their manuscripts. Publishing a book is extremely difficult! The level of commitment must be high both on your part and on that of the publisher, meaning you *really* want to work with the publisher and the publisher *really* likes your book.

With a full-length manuscript, never-failing persistence will serve you well. Keep polishing and sending out your book until it finds a home. If, after submitting for several years, you feel better about tabling the manuscript than the choices that remain for publishing it, that's fine. But until that day, don't let the rejections get you down. See chapter 7 for more on small press writers' publication journeys. These journeys take time.

As you learn to roll with the punches of rejection, it may be helpful to consider the lesson of Kim Liao's viral *Lit Hub* article, "Why You Should Aim for 100 Rejections a Year." Liao recommends setting your submitting goals in terms of rejections rather than acceptances, since we simply cannot control the outcome of our submissions. In this framework, receiving a response that declines your work is still meaningful. Liao writes, "I see rejection as a conversation: for every piece that is rejected, at least one other person read it, thought about it, and really considered whether it would be a good fit for publication.

What's more, it's a conversation between two minds that truly love literature, as the financial margins of journals and small presses are slimmer than the sheaf of pages that I carry with me each day to revise before going to my day job."

Liao asks us to tune in to the process of submitting rather than the result, taking seriously the interpersonal connection beneath the surface of submission managers and form letters. Rejection is not simply rejection: it is an essential part of the writing journey.

How to Follow Up on Positive Rejections

There is magic in an editor reading your work and, even if they can't publish it, making an effort to support your writing. Positive rejections are an investment in your future, a way of saying you're on the right track and it's only a matter of time.

Positive rejections also give you a leg up in the submissions process. If you mention in your cover letter that you have received an encouraging rejection from the publication where you're submitting, editors take note of this fact and pay special attention to your work. This could mean the submission goes directly to a senior editor, skipping the first round of readers. It could simply mean your piece gets a more sympathetic read. Either way, always include a note in the first line of your cover letter if you have received an encouraging rejection from that publication in the past. See chapter 5 for advice on how to phrase this.

The cover letter is only part of your potential engagement with publications that have positively rejected your writing. When resubmitting to a venue that has responded encouragingly to your work, be mindful about your submissions process as well. This is your chance to send your writing to someone who will look especially closely at it! Treat the editors with respect and thoughtfulness, do additional research on the publication, and submit writing you really believe fits their taste.

Identity and Equity in the Writing World

The intersection of your identities will affect your experience of submitting and publishing as well. It's no secret that the world of publishing is very white. Accounts of racial inequity in publishing have focused on the Big 5 houses, but the same problems extend into the world of small presses and literary magazines. These inequities are not limited to race. The writing world often decenters the experiences of LGBTQ+ people, women, and disabled people, limits access to writers without generational wealth, and marginalizes writers with identities that can't be monetized or aren't legible to the mainstream. As a literary community, we have begun to recognize these problems, but that doesn't mean we have solved them.

It's essential to work together with literary magazines and small presses toward the literary landscape we want to see in the world. If you're a writer who is marginalized or excluded from mainstream publishing, community and self-protection may factor into your decisions about where to submit. Finding support with literary organizations can be one way to navigate the literary landscape with a sense of community. Cave Canem, for example, provides a literary home for Black poets. Kundiman supports Asian American writers. Lambda Literary advocates for and gives yearly awards to LGBTQ+ writers. See appendix B for a more complete list of identity-based literary organizations.

Many publications also focus on writers from specific communities. Examples include *Callaloo*, a journal publishing writers in the African diaspora; Arte Público Press, which publishes Latinx writers; *Mizna*, a magazine publishing Arab writers; Kaya Press, which publishes AAPI writers; Abalone Mountain Press, which publishes Native writers; and *Foglifter*, a magazine focused on LGBTQ+ writing. Other presses are driven by a mission, such as Dorothy, a feminist press publishing mostly women; AK Press, an anarchist press; and Radix Media, a worker-owned press prioritizing marginalized voices. Publication opportunities are not limited to these venues, of course. You can find a trusted home in many publications, although it is always good to do your research about who they are publishing and whether you will feel at home in their pages or catalog. The number of publications and opportunities that are run by, or thoughtfully supportive of, marginalized writers is increasing by the day.

If you're a writer who has been traditionally centered in publishing, it's equally important to consider the role of your identities in your writing life. White writers, especially white men, receive unspoken privileges as writers, including the baseline assumption that their stories are worth telling. Familial wealth allows certain writers easy access to the time, space, and education that support their writing. Nondisabled writers don't have to worry about their stories being labeled as "inspiring," and writers born in the United States don't have to contend with stereotyped immigrant narratives. In general, a sense of belonging and comfort in literary spaces is easier for privileged writers to come by.

That's why, if you're a writer with privilege, it's good to use that privilege to question the status quo. One way to do this is to support small presses and literary magazines whose publishing practices respond to these problems. You can hold accountable the venues where you publish and encourage them to work toward equity. Even more important, you can envision your own writing as part of a larger conversation in which you are not the center. As a privileged writer, you have something to say. But it's not the *only* thing, and it may not even be the most important thing. When giving interviews or readings of your work, for example, you can directly acknowledge your debt to marginalized writers whose writing makes your writing possible. In your conversations with fellow writers, you can make thoughtful decisions about how much space to occupy.

Each person's identities and experiences intersect in complicated ways. You might incur some privileges in the publishing world while being marginalized in other respects. The same goes for editors. When working with editors and other writers, keep in mind that these intersections are always at play.

Your navigation of identity and privilege in your writing life will be unique. The most important thing is to remember who you are, believe in your writing, and be thoughtful about how your work fits (or should fit) in the larger literary landscape.

Know Thyself

Your experiences and identities may also inform your strategy for submitting. Editors regularly note the disparity in submissions they receive across gender lines, for example. Men tend to flood the submission portals. As per the influential VIDA Count, men are also overrepresented in the proportion of genders published in literary magazines. These kinds of disparities persist, even though parts of the literary world are working to change them, and it's worth thinking about how they affect your submission practice.

In the early years of my writing life, my own submissions

followed this pattern, influenced by my experiences as a privileged white man. I was much too quick to submit. I would write, quickly revise, and then submit in a flurry of self-confidence. Only after a few weeks — and many rejections — would I return to what I had written, realizing I simply hadn't spent enough time on it to be sharing it with editors.

After a while, I realized this pattern didn't result in writing I felt good about. It wasn't respectful of editors either. I taught myself to pause the first (and second and third) time I wanted to submit. I used those moments to step away from the piece I was writing. For a few weeks I let it breathe. Then I returned to revisions. When I had done as much as I possibly could, I stepped away again. After a few more weeks, I returned to revisions.

Only when I had spent many months in this process — and when I couldn't find anything else I wanted to change about it, even after taking time away — did I judge the work to be ready. I learned to distrust my instantaneous confidence that came with the act of writing. I learned to rely on my view of the work over time.

Do you tend to be overconfident in your work, sharing it before you're ready? If so, tap the brakes when you first decide you want to submit. Wait a month, and then return to your piece. Make sure you've given your writing as much time as you possibly can before asking someone else to give their time to it.

On the other hand, do you tend to be overprotective of your writing? Do you continue to tweak and refine long after others say it's done? Are you hesitant to begin submitting it? In that case, consider sending your work out earlier. Changing that last little comma or that last turn of phrase might not be worth it if it means never letting your work see the light.

Work toward knowing yourself as a submitter. Allow this self-knowledge to be both a corrective and an inspiration, pointing you toward the practices that will help you be a more well-rounded submitter and writer.

Treat Editors with Respect

Your submission strategy will be incomplete, finally, without a healthy dose of respect for the editors to whom you are submitting. It can be easy to feel, when clicking Submit on your latest piece of writing, as if you are simply sending it into the void, only to hear back when the wheel of fortune has spun and decided your fate.

In fact, there *is* an actual person on the other side of the transom. That person wants to find something that really speaks to them, a piece that is inspired and revised and fully thought out, a piece that springs from a deep emotional place and a committed writing practice. That person is the editor, and they are as real as you.

Remembering this fact helps motivate me when I am finalizing my manuscript and planning my submissions. Knowing somebody is *actually* going to read your writing can motivate you to:

- keep revising (and revising and revising) until your manuscript is capital-F Finished, so that you can truly stand behind what you have created.
- get a strong sense of the publication, including whether the piece you're submitting is a good fit.
- draft a cover letter that is thoughtful about editors' tastes and respectful of their time.
- be patient with editors after you've submitted, knowing they're doing their best to consider the many submissions they receive.

Finally, think about how long you wait before sending another submission to the same publication. I would not advise immediately resubmitting to a publication the same day you receive a rejection letter from them. Some journals will explicitly request that you wait a few months before submitting again. Even for those that don't, giving them time to catch up on other submissions (and giving yourself time to perfect your writing) is a good way to respect their editorial work.

Your Personal Strategy

As mentioned earlier, tiered submissions take the guesswork out of submissions. Set up your tiers, submit to them in order, and you will always know what's next in your submission process.

But how do you set up your tiers? How do you decide which publishers you want to publish with? It's hard to answer these questions right out of the gate. It takes time and experience to assemble a personalized list of publications you'd like to submit to. You will likely fine-tune your tiers over the course of your submitting life, as your goals shift and your understanding of the literary landscape grows.

When assembling your tiers, return to your goals from chapter 1. Remind yourself why you're doing this! Then select the publications that are most likely to help you achieve those goals.

What follows are several possible strategies for structuring your tiers. You can mix and match these as desired, as well as add your own strategies.

Prestige

Prestigious publications have an undeniably magnetic draw. It feels good to have your publications recognized by your friends, and it can help you gain wider notoriety as a writer to publish in venues with a good reputation. These achievements can fuel your writing, since they are more likely to result in paid writing opportunities and the expectation that you will write more.

There's nothing wrong, therefore, with aiming for prestigious venues. But it's always wise to remember the trade-offs. The more well-known a venue is, the longer response times are and the lower the likelihood of acceptance. If you're aiming high, you should be prepared to wait a very long time to hear back about your writing and to submit many times, perhaps over many years, before receiving an acceptance.

It is also wise to see prestigious publications as more than just rubber stamps of approval. Like other publications, they are part of a conversation. There is community and shared sensibility, even at the top. If you're submitting to these venues, make sure you've read the writing they publish and you see your own writing as part of that conversation. How would you define the personal resonance — the writerly sense of connection — that draws you to these venues, aside from their prominence?

A submitting strategy that focuses on prestige makes sense if you want to use publication to advance your career. You will likely have worked on your writing for many years before you have success with this strategy. You will feel at the top of your game, having arrived at the point where you know your work could (and should!) appear alongside the major names in contemporary writing.

Working Your Way Up

What if you don't feel ready to submit to prestigious publications? What if you don't want to wait forever for a response to your submission? Maybe you want to get some publications under your belt before trying the best-known magazines. Maybe you want to focus on building literary community during the earlier stages of submitting.

"Working your way up" means starting small and following your submission practice as it grows. You may eventually want to publish with prestigious journals and presses, but for now your goals are to see your work appear in the world and to lay the groundwork for your further writing and its publication.

When following this strategy, begin by submitting to small and/or less exclusive literary magazines. Choose them based on your preference for each publication rather than on their level of prestige. As you connect with publications that feature writing you like — and as they connect with your writing — you'll grow more confident. You will begin to find your place in the literary world without relying on prestige to define you.

Eventually, you may begin to submit to more prestigious publications. This will feel like a natural progression, an act of growing alongside your writing. If and when the time comes, you will already feel grounded as a writer and submitter. You'll have been publishing your writing for a while now. Prestige is just the cherry on top.

Online or Local Community

You can also choose a submission strategy that puts community at the forefront. This strategy recognizes the importance of the specific editors you publish with, the particular readers you write for, and the writers you connect with in the real world. The community you write toward — and ultimately become a part of — could be anywhere, in person or online.

If you want to focus on in-person community, submit to magazines, presses, and literary organizations in your geographical area. Attend readings. Buy local zines. Help assemble chapbooks with a local publisher. The community writing workshops listed in appendix B can help you connect with local writers and organizations, but they are only a beginning. In-person writing groups, reading series, and literary festivals abound. Publishing locally is a way to stay grounded and connected with these active literary communities.

The internet helps you connect even more widely, even though it can feel more diffuse than in-person community. Online clusters of writers and editors often form through loosely related sets of publications across the country. Cadres of writers and publications create ongoing conversations on social media. Members of these loose communities might occasionally see each other in person, but the internet is the basis of their relationship. Through online connections, you can expand your reach to writers who work in the same subgenre as you, who write about a related subject area, or who share your identity or experiences.

To find the in-person or online communities that are meaningful to you, begin with writers you already like and publications you already know. Follow the breadcrumbs: Where have those writers published? Who else have those publications featured? Where do these interconnected threads lead you? Simply by being enthusiastic about — and submitting to — the same publications, you might become part of a loose community of writers.

Celebrate the simple act of community that comes with publication. Read your fellow contributors' work. Reach out to them over social media. Interview them about their forthcoming books. Connect with them at a literary festival or a local coffee shop, if they live near you. Sign up for their newsletter. Appreciate the threads that connect you with a group of writers publishing their writing together.

Personalized, Specific Goals

You can also make room in your strategy for your specific, very personal goals. For example, I tend to be attentive to the graphic design of the literary magazines and presses where I publish. It's important to me that my writing is presented in a way that is professional, eye-catching, and readable. My decisions about where to submit, therefore, are highly influenced by the look of each publication.

Your aims will likely differ. Maybe it would mean a lot to you to publish in the first literary magazine you ever read. Maybe you have three bucket-list publications that published your favorite writer early in their career. Maybe you want to connect with a certain editor because you follow them on social media and are inspired by their approach to writing. Maybe you want to win prizes. Maybe you want to maximize payment. Maybe you want to focus on online publications, since those will be the most widely accessible.

Don't be shy about choosing where to submit based on what is meaningful to you. It's easy to get caught up in where you "should" submit. Instead, submit where you really *want* to, even if your goals are strange and secret and only you understand them.

The Joy of Submitting

All this talk of strategy and goal setting can feel overly calculated, especially when we are submitting writing that is close to our heart. Our writing blooms from a place of passion and intuition, so why should the process of working toward publication be so cut-and-dried?

That's why it makes sense to choose a strategy that prioritizes joy. You can still make a plan, use tiered submissions, and be smart about how you're sending out your writing. While doing all this, you can decide where to submit on the basis of sheer enthusiasm. When you find a publication you like, even if you don't know why you like it, embrace your intuition. Welcome the parts of submitting that light you up.

Remember: submitting your writing should give back to your writing. At its best, submitting can inspire us. Following your desire and intuition is a great way to ensure that the inspiration you need comes through.

• • •

In practice, you will likely use a combination of several strategies to submit your writing. You might work your way up with most of your submissions but take a chance on prestige when you are submitting the writing you are most proud of. You might target local community for certain submissions while building a widespread online community with the rest of them. You might allow pinches of each strategy to influence your decision-making, resulting in a holistic submitting sensibility.

You might also be submitting multiple types of writing, which leads to different strategic choices for each. You might send researched personal essays to prestigious national journals while focusing your poetry submissions on small DIY publishing outfits. You might target mainstream literary magazines for most of your short fiction while branching out into innovative and genre-agnostic publishers for your edgiest stories.

When it comes to books, I have seen many writers publish novels with a Big 5 press, then publish poetry or less-commercial prose with a small press. Successful authors often have deep community roots in addition to their prestigious qualifications. You don't have to choose between pursuing recognizable literary achievement and supporting your favorite writing communities. You can do both!

Similarly, there is no need to limit yourself to one style of submitting. Allow your strategies to respond to your writing, your needs, and your hopes. Forget about what you "should" do. Choose the path that keeps you writing.

Writing Prompt

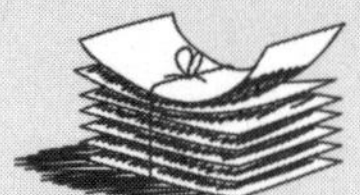

Brainstorm your personal submission strategy.

Which of the submission strategies above would you like to practice? Which strategies might you combine? Are there any strategies you don't see here that you'd like to try?

Most importantly, how will you practice these strategies in a way that gives energy and inspiration back to your writing?

When you've finished writing, take a minute to read what you've written. Envision yourself taking the steps you have described. Next, imagine yourself having success with these plans.

What does it feel like to achieve your goals? Let that feeling fuel your submission process, and keep it in mind with each step you take.

Once you've decided on your submission strategy, it's time to *share* your submission plans. This part of submitting often flies under the radar, but it's essential: you need to get support for the process. Sharing your intentions helps you step fully and confidently into the act of submitting your writing. Start by talking to a friend, a romantic partner, a colleague, or a fellow writer — anyone who is willing to listen to and support you on your submitting journey. Share with them your hopes as well as your struggles and worries. Ask if they have any words of encouragement.

Next, make a plan for regular accountability and support. Some writers join writing groups that meet weekly, monthly, or irregularly. Writers in these groups read each other's writing, make comments and suggestions for revision, and share experiences of the writing life. They also talk about submitting and publishing. A trusted circle of writers is a great place to share your successes and struggles in working toward publication, and it gives you the opportunity to learn from others' experiences.

Some writers also benefit from classes that focus on working toward publication, which are offered at many community writing workshops, both in person and online (see appendix B). Additionally, submission parties, in which writers gather to submit their writing together, are a fun, celebratory way to stay accountable as a submitter and to share submitting practices. You can set a date for a submission party yourself and invite your writer friends, either regularly or as a one-time event.

If you prefer a more informal approach, you could ask a fellow writer to meet each month and talk about submissions together; you could share your submission experiences on social media; or you could keep a submission diary that's just for you but that still gives you the feeling of vocalizing your experience with submitting.

The crucial thing is that you find a strategy that will support you throughout your journey as a submitter. Setting aside a designated time for checking in holds you accountable and keeps you grounded during the difficult times. We need to share our successes, failures, and struggles. The more you talk about submitting and publishing, the more it becomes a real part of your life.

5

The Cover Letter

The cover letter is a genre all its own. Given that it's the only thing accompanying your submission, the cover letter can feel like the key, your one chance to make your case. This makes it easy to obsess over cover letters, trying to make them as convincing as we possibly can.

In reality, the key is your submission itself. Your writing is where you should direct the most energy when preparing for submission. If you're going to edit obsessively, edit your poem, essay, story, or book.

The cover letter should be relatively quick and easy, especially if you're using a cover letter template (see chapter 3). But it does need to do a few essential things. A cover letter's main goals are to:

- communicate your interest in the venue where you are submitting.
- present you as a reasonable, thoughtful writer whom editors would be able to work with easily.
- give the basic facts about your piece: genre, word count, and special circumstances surrounding the writing such as a previous positive rejection, a themed issue, or your relationship with one of the editors.

- honestly represent who you are through your bio.
- display gratitude to the editors for reading your work.

This doesn't sound like a tall order, but it means you have to find a balance between overdoing it and underdoing it, between saying too much and not saying enough. A successful cover letter walks that thin line. Instead of convincing editors to accept a piece, it allows them to consider your writing on their own terms. While it describes your accomplishments, it does not brag or seem over the top. Being professional in a cover letter means offering what you have clearly and concisely, then stepping back to let the editors do their work.

I want to be clear that when I say *cover letters* I am talking about a very specific thing: the short letter that typically accompanies submissions of fiction, poetry, and creative nonfiction to literary magazines and small presses. In the days of submissions via mail, cover letters were a printed letter that literally covered (went on top of) your submission. With most online submissions, you enter a cover letter in a box alongside your uploaded submission. With email submissions, you write your cover letter in the body of your email, with your submission attached. Cover letters are the first thing an editor sees when they open your submission. They are always accompanied by a full manuscript, with the understanding that the editor is primarily evaluating the manuscript itself. The cover letter is an informative supplement, that delicate dance between introducing yourself and getting out of the way.

I am *not* talking about pitch letters, which precede certain nonfiction submissions. Online venues that publish personal essays; timely takes on culture, literature, and media; and list articles often ask for pitches. You typically send a pitch letter before you have even written an article, in hopes that a publication will pay you to write it. Fiction, poetry, and creative nonfiction are not usually submitted in this fashion, although some forms of creative nonfiction (like personal essays) are occasionally submitted this way. Pitch letters usually apply to articles with an argument or a reported element.

I am also not talking about query letters to agents, which are an entirely different genre. Query letters act as a pitch for your book, focusing on its suitability for the marketplace and trying to convince agents to read your manuscript or proposal. Query letters are relatively persuasive and market focused. A cover letter, on the other hand, does not need to make an argument. You should assume that your manuscript will be read regardless of what you write in your cover letter.

Cover letters are not separate from market forces, of course, and they may subtly pitch or persuade. The unique task of cover letters is to briefly do these things while ultimately allowing your writing to stand on its own.

How Important Is the Cover Letter, Really?

In an ideal world, every piece of writing would get the same shot at publication, whether the writer is well-known or has never been published before. Editors would look at the cover letter only after they have decided whether to publish a piece. How you present yourself would have nothing to do with whether you receive an acceptance or a rejection.

In reality, editors see your cover letter immediately, whether or not they want to. This is simply how Submittable is set up. When I first began reading submissions for a literary magazine, I was told to ignore the cover letters and go straight to the writing. Despite this, I couldn't help glancing at the cover letter first. It was right there in front of me, and I wanted to know whose writing I was about to read.

Perhaps it is reasonable for an editor to expect an introduction when they are about to read your writing. But the tough part is when the cover letter begins to sway their opinion before they've even looked at the submission itself. If a cover letter is warm and to the point, with several books listed in the bio, it's easy for an editor to lean toward the possibility of acceptance. If a cover letter is cracking jokes or trying to sound impressive, an editor might expect writing that is on the newer side. If a letter is curt or unthoughtful, an editor might feel hesitant to publish the writer, regardless of the writing itself.

Consider this case from an editor's point of view: A relatively well-known writer submits work that is a hard maybe for publication. If it were coming from a writer without any published books, it would be easy to send a positive rejection. But based on who wrote it, the readers and editors question their own taste. The writer must know what they're doing, right? After all, look at their accomplishments. The editors accept the piece, and they get the benefit of a well-known writer in their table of contents.

Here's another possibility: A writer sends a cover letter with a three-paragraph bio, touting publication in hundreds of literary magazines and listing every one of them. The writer's tone is less than humble, maybe even a little arrogant. The editors like the submission itself, but they are hesitant. Do they really want to be another name in the writer's laundry list of publications? Whether or not they accept the submission, the cover letter is working against the writer.

So the answer is, yes, the cover letter matters. It's not everything, but it is *something*. It's worth taking the time to construct your cover letter thoughtfully. Be brief, generous, and grateful. Make it easy to accept your submission.

The Parts of a Cover Letter

Salutation

In the first line of your cover letter, you already have a chance to show you've done your research on the publication you are submitting to. Find the names of the editors and include them in your salutation. For a more formal submission, you can use the editor's full name, which helps you avoid applying inaccurate honorifics:

Dear Firstname Lastname,

For a more casual tone, including when you have a preexisting relationship with the literary magazine or press where you are submitting, you can simply use the editor's first name:

Dear Firstname,

A personalized salutation lets editors know you've taken the time to find out who they are; it also bridges the impersonal gap created by submission managers. You are acknowledging editors as real people, which will remind them you are a real person, too.

Address the editors of the genre you're submitting to. Find the fiction editor(s) if you are submitting fiction, nonfiction editor(s) if you are submitting nonfiction, poetry editor(s) if you are submitting poetry, and so on. If there are no specific genre editors, address the person (or people) at the top of the masthead.

You can find the names of editors on the masthead or the

About page of most publications' websites. If their names aren't available, it is fine to write, "Dear nonfiction editors," "Dear fiction editors," or "Dear poetry editors."

Introduction and Essential Info

In chapter 3, I recommend maintaining a cover letter template you can copy and paste into each submission. The introductory paragraph of your cover letter, however, is one paragraph you can't standardize. It will change based on what you are submitting, where you are submitting, and your relationship with the publication.

That said, you will likely develop a set of stock phrases you can return to over time in this paragraph of the cover letter. You can include these phrases in your cover letter template, if it's helpful to you.

The introductory paragraph of the cover letter should include the following information, in roughly this order. You do not have to include all this information. If a line doesn't apply to you, leave it out.

- **Positive rejection?** Inform the editors if you have received a positive rejection from them in the recent past. This should be the first line of your cover letter, after the salutation. You want to make sure the editors see it.
  Example: Thank you very much for your encouraging words about the last submission I sent.
  Example: Thank you for your kind comments on my last two submissions and your invitation to submit again.
- **Connection?** Inform the editors if you have a personal relationship to the publication or an explicit invitation to submit from one of the editors.

Example: I appreciated getting to meet you this spring and am grateful for your invitation to submit.

Example: I am a former contributor from issue ____, and I thought this new essay might also be right for your pages.

- **The logistics.** Give the basic details of the piece. This information should be in every cover letter.

  Title: For a short story, poem, or essay, put the title in quotation marks. Book titles should be italicized, without quotation marks.

  Genre: Say whether you are submitting a short story, essay, or poems. You can be more specific, using subcategories such as flash fiction and lyric essay, but this is usually not necessary. If you are sending multiple shorter pieces, such as poems or flash fiction, let them know how many you are sending.

  Word Count: Round to the next 100 words.

  Example: Thank you very much for considering "Title," a 2,800-word short story.

  Example: I am writing to submit three poems, "Title 1," "Title 2," and "Title 3."

- **Your (or your writing's) relationship to the publication.** The first paragraph is also an opportunity to mention the qualities of the publication that motivated you to submit. You only need to include this if you have something unique and substantive to say. Generalized praise for a publication is not necessary. You can also mention upcoming themed issues that are relevant to your piece.

  Example: I am submitting this to you in particular because of your magazine's focus on ____. This essay is interested in ____.

Example: As a longtime subscriber, I thought this might be a good fit for your consistent mix of ____ and ____.

Example: I thought these poems might be a fit for your ____ issue, since they revolve around ____.

- **Background.** Give context for the piece of writing you are submitting. This can be helpful when you want editors to understand your depth of engagement with the subject matter or personal relationship to the material.

  Example: This short story is part of my collection in progress, ____, which tells the story of ____.

  Example: These poems grow out of my time in ____, where I lived recently on a ____ fellowship.

Less is more when it comes to cover letters, and the introductory paragraph is no exception. The main job of this paragraph is to introduce your submission to the editors who will be reading it and remark on any special circumstances. You're aiming for connection, not comprehensiveness. Two to three sentences is plenty.

Bio

The author biography, which comes after the introductory paragraph of the cover letter, is also a balancing act. On the one hand, you want to convey your seriousness about writing and accomplishments. On the other, you don't want to exhaust your reader with a laundry list of publications and achievements. Include the highlights of your writing life and not much more. Shoot for a tone that is both concise and confident in your commitment to writing.

This means that if you've published in fifteen lit mags, truncate the list to the four or five most impressive ones. If you have an MFA, include it, but leave out your undergraduate degree. You can also include publications you help edit, literary organizations you contribute to, reading series you organize, and other forms of literary involvement. Information like how long you have been writing is not necessary. The primary goal of the author bio is to place you in literary context and to help editors understand where you are in your writing career.

Here are several templates you can use when constructing your bio. You will likely add to, subtract from, and otherwise alter these templates:

If you have no publications:

> I live in ____, where I work as a ____. This would be my first published ____.

If you have a few publications:

> My fiction/nonfiction/poetry has appeared in ____ and ____. I live in ____, where I work as a ____.

If you have several publications and a couple of fellowships or residencies, along with additional involvement in the literary community:

> My fiction/nonfiction/poetry has appeared in ____, ____, ____, and ____, among others, and has been supported by ____ and ____. I live in ____, where I run the reading series ____.

If you have a book, several publications, an MFA, and editorial positions or other forms of literary involvement:

> I am the author of ____. My fiction/nonfiction/poetry has also appeared in ____, ____, ____, and ____, among others. I am an editor for ____, and I run a local writing organization, ____. I received my MFA from ____ and live in ____.

These templates are written in the first person because *I* flows better in a cover letter, but you can use third-person for a more formal approach. Some submission guidelines ask explicitly for third-person. If you are using a third-person bio in your cover letter, I would precede the bio with, "Here is a short biography."

As you write and publish, your bio will inevitably change. Keep updating it in your cover letter template by adding new publications while revising for concision. Reading other authors' bios, whether they're on books or in the contributor section of literary journals, is a great way to fine-tune your bio-writing sensibility. Aim for a few strong sentences that highlight your relationship with the literary landscape so far.

Sign-Off

The sign-off paragraph isn't strictly necessary, but I include it to make the cover letter more generous and less curt. For me, this paragraph is an opportunity to express my gratitude to the editors for reading what I've submitted.

A few examples:

- Thank you for considering ____.

- Thank you again for considering ____. I look forward to hearing from you.
- Thank you for your consideration, and I hope you're doing well.

I use the last example only if I personally know the editors. Additionally, you can use this paragraph to inform editors you are sending a simultaneous submission, which some publications ask for in their submission guidelines.

Valediction

Keep it simple. "Sincerely" or "All best" will do the job. Sign off with your full name, since you've likely addressed the editors with theirs, unless you know them personally.

• • •

Tailor these templates to your own style, but don't worry about making them exciting, interesting, or funny. As with formatting, a cover letter should be largely unremarkable, which makes room for the submission itself to shine. Remind editors that you are grateful for their work, that you know the rules of submissions, and that you are a real person who would be nice to work with. Then press Submit!

Cover Letters for a Book Submission

There's one type of cover letter that does merit more sustained attention: the cover letter for a book. If you are submitting a full manuscript, it is likely the culmination of years of writing. Your heart is on every page, and you are on the cusp of the next big step in your writing life. It's one thing to have your name in the table of contents of a literary magazine. It's another thing altogether to have your name on the title page of a book you wrote.

Cover letters for book-length manuscripts help editors get a sense of you as a person, writer, and literary citizen, and they communicate why you believe their press is right for your book. This is particularly important because you're asking for a major commitment from editors when you submit a book. They'll invest months of their time and energy into publishing you, and you'll work closely with them on everything from editing to promotion. Some small presses publish as few as two books a year, and many publish fewer than five or ten. Each book they publish becomes a representation of their press. Choosing who to publish is the beginning of a long-term relationship.

Doing your research, therefore, is essential to submitting to a small press. This research, detailed in chapter 2, will help you make decisions about which presses to submit to. It will also inform the introductory paragraph of your cover letter. This introductory paragraph may even expand into multiple paragraphs when you are submitting a book.

In these paragraphs, you should communicate not only your interest in publishing with the press but also a short description of your book and how it intertwines with the publisher's catalog and mission. Has the press published a book that has been influential to you as a writer? Do they have a mission that matters to you? What do you admire about the press and their catalog? What made you want to submit this specific book to them? Your answers to questions like these will help the editors understand how you would fit in their catalog.

If you mention your personal connection to the press, make sure it is coming from a genuine place. You don't *always* have to say something complimentary, because you can't have read multiple books from every single publisher. If you have done only light research on that press in preparation for submitting, it's better to say less.

These introductory paragraphs are also an opportunity to include a description of your book that suits the publisher to whom you're submitting. This description should include word count, genre, and title, but it should also go beyond these basic details. You might give a pitchy description of your book's plot. You might describe the book's genre and style, if the press is attentive to matters of form. You might describe your intended audience, or your book's relationship to the publisher's mission.

How you tailor these paragraphs, of course, depends on where you are submitting. A chapbook micropress, for example, might appreciate a cover letter that is personal, DIY, and not too pitchy. A press whose mission addresses a specific community might be interested in your and your writing's relationship to that community. A large indie press might expect a cover letter that is more like a query letter, in which you emphasize the salable qualities of your book, alongside a bio with your most impressive achievements. Communicate in a way that fits each publisher's style, catalog, and goals.

At the end of the day, your cover letter builds a connection. It tells editors why you've submitted to them and why you believe they might want to publish your book. You're showing that you speak a shared language. You're offering your contribution to a conversation they have already begun.

Submitting to Contests

If you're submitting to a book contest, however, you can take a much simpler approach to the cover letter. Most contests are judged anonymously, and cover letters, if they are read at all, are read after the fact.

That said, don't entirely ignore the document. Contest cover letters can still be a good place to communicate your interest in publishing with a press. Including a strong bio also motivates editors to take your work seriously and think of your role in the larger literary context, if they are on the fence about publishing you.

Some book contests even operate on a graduated system, where finalists are evaluated for publication even if they do not win. Keep an eye out for contests like these, because they effectively offer multiple routes to publication. Be thoughtful about your cover letter in these cases, as the editors might read it closely after all.

Following Up

Waiting for a response can be the hardest part of submitting your writing. Small presses and literary magazines rarely get back to you in the amount of time stated in their guidelines, which means you have no clue as to when you will receive a response. This might lead you to ask when you should follow up after sending a submission. Should you write to a publication if you don't hear from them for six months? For a year? Should you follow up at all?

In my experience, follow-up emails rarely influence how quickly your submission is considered. Editors read submissions in the order they're received unless they have a very good reason to skip the line. Even if you're not likely to speed up the reading process, however, you have the right to follow up after a publication has kept your submission longer than the stated response time in their guidelines.

There are times when following up can be helpful, even if it doesn't get you a quicker answer. One of these is when you've submitted to a venue you particularly want to publish with. Sending a follow-up message after a few months can be a helpful way of reiterating your interest. You can also follow up if waiting on a submission is preventing you from taking the next step in your submission strategy. You don't want to wait forever, and an update from the editors could help you figure out your next move. There's no need to follow up with contest submissions, however. Contests are usually evaluated based on a preexisting schedule, which means that every entry receives a response at the designated time.

If you do choose to follow up, use a gracious tone that does not pressure editors. Here's an example follow-up letter:

> Dear ____,
>
> I'm writing to follow up on ____, a ____ I submitted in ____. I was wondering if you could provide an update on the status of the piece.
>
> I know it takes time to consider the many manuscripts you receive. Thank you very much for your continued consideration.
>
> All best,

If you have a specific reason for following up now, you could insert a sentence in the middle of the first paragraph stating what has prompted you to write.

Withdrawing Your Writing

The last piece of potential communication between you and a publication (aside from acceptance, discussed in chapter 8) is the withdrawal letter. Following up to withdraw a piece is essential when it is accepted by another venue. Doing so is common courtesy, and it ensures that editors won't spend their time reading a piece that is no longer available.

Publications that use Submittable have a Withdraw function you can click on to take your submission out of the queue. It includes a small text box where you can let the editors know why you're withdrawing your work. For publications that do not use Submittable, sending an email to the genre editor or managing editor is fine. Most publications include instructions about how to withdraw your submission in their submission guidelines.

While you might see withdrawing a piece as an afterthought, it can actually serve as a building block for your relationship with a publication. A withdrawal subtly communicates that your work is in demand: it's been accepted, after all! If you communicate this with grace, the editors may have a positive impression of you when you submit in the future.

I usually take the time to write a brief but polite note when withdrawing my writing so the editors know I appreciate their considering my work:

> Dear ____,
>
> I'm writing to withdraw ____, which I submitted in ____, as it was just accepted at another literary magazine.
>
> Thanks so much for your consideration, and my apologies for any inconvenience.
>
> All best,

If it's a publication you're particularly fond of, you can even add a personal note of apology after the first sentence, as well as a statement to the effect of, "I look forward to sending you another submission in the future."

Beyond the Cover Letter: Connections and Side Doors in Submissions

Most of the writers who receive acceptances have submitted through the front door, using only their cover letter to introduce their writing. They've been offered publication based on the writing itself, only secondarily bolstered by their cover letter or writerly status. Some people underestimate the "slush pile," but don't let them fool you: submissions are the heart of small press and literary magazine publishing. It's what makes this literary landscape so lively, innovative, and full of writerly promise.

That said, writers do sometimes find publication through the side door. In these cases, the cover letter is not the only introduction to the writer's work; other interactions and communications have already laid the groundwork for their submission. It's important to acknowledge this fact rather than pretending that publishing is a strict meritocracy. Publishing is a community. Knowing or being connected to someone can have a meaningful effect on the results of the submission process.

This fact can sometimes feel like nepotism. Indeed, the weight of relationships in decisions about publication can preserve long-standing power imbalances. Insularity protects people who have influence, making it difficult for new writers to break in.

Other times, however, writerly relationships act as fertile soil for writing that isn't yet recognized as groundbreaking. Groundbreaking writing needs support to flourish on its own terms. By supporting writers we know and care about, we carve a space outside of "good" or "bad" writing. We build communities of thought and imagination that otherwise would never have the chance to flourish.

It's up to you to invest in the writing communities you believe in. If that makes it more likely that editors will publish you, it's at least partially because they know your work is intentionally speaking to them.

All this is to say there are constructive things about the side doors, legs up, and connections that inform responses to submissions. You can think of these as addendums to the cover letter: additional sources of information that help editors make a decision. Some feel fairer than others. It's good to remember that, if you keep writing and publishing, you may ultimately be in a position of not only receiving but also giving favors. It will then be up to you to shape the literary world as you want to see it.

What follows are a few possible connections, outside of a cover letter, that could influence how your submission is read.

- **Relationship with an editor through previous submissions.** If you receive enough positive rejections over the years from the same editor, particularly if they include personal notes, you may develop a rapport with them. This is rewarding for both the editor and writer. The editor gets to cultivate and encourage a writer whose work they admire, and you get the gift of positive feedback on your work. These relationships can eventually bloom into publication, if you submit the right piece of writing.

- **Relationship with an editor in real life.** The longer you participate in literary community, the more likely you are to know an editor at a magazine or press. Editors are likely to give your work a closer read if you have met in real life. But you shouldn't expect your relationships with editors to result in publication. Editors can tell if you're treating them instrumentally. Instead, remember that your literary relationships are ends in themselves, rewarding because of your shared interests and not because of what you can get out of them.
- **Solicitations.** I was shocked the first time I received an email asking me, personally, to submit my work to a publication. How did the editor know who I was? Had they really read my work and liked it? If your work has been published, you never know when the editor of a different publication might find it and ask if you have more. Not all publications rely on solicitations. For those that do, it is a way of supplementing their submissions queue with writing they know will fit their editorial vision. Solicitations do not guarantee publication, but editors turning down a solicited piece of writing is (or should be) rare.
- **Unexpected byways.** Once you begin to publish your writing, unexpected opportunities may arise. An editor may share their email address so you don't have to go through the submission portal the next time you submit. Another editor might request a look at your full-length manuscript after they publish an excerpt in their literary magazine. Yet another editor might refer you to a different publication, giving you permission to use their name in your cover letter. The more you submit, the more often these opportunities will come up.

• • •

Regardless of where you are in your publishing journey, there's always a person on the other end reading your cover letter. Submission is an act of communication. If you keep working at it, your act of communication will lead to more communication, which will lead to finding more publications and meeting more people, which will lead to building community. Eventually, writing a cover letter will feel less like throwing your hat in a ring and more like continuing a conversation you're already a part of.

6

Behind the Scenes

After you press Submit, take a deep breath. Celebrate the fact that your words are now out there, being read. You can let go of your writing, at least for a few days. Take a break. Think about what you want to write next.

While you wait, this chapter will help you understand what is happening behind the scenes of literary magazines and small presses. The story will be different for every publication. This basic overview, however, will allow you to grasp the ins and outs a manuscript goes through when being considered for publication.

This chapter may also inform your submission strategy. For many writers, becoming a reader or editor at a literary publication is a time-tested way to improve both your writing and your submission process. If you have a realistic understanding of how editors evaluate your work, you can submit in ways that fit those editorial practices.

Just don't worry *too* much about what is happening to your submission. Literary magazines and small presses don't work on the same timeline as writerly anxiety. Once you've submitted, try your best to have faith in your writing. Accept the inevitable ups and downs. Then, when you're ready, start writing something new.

How Literary Magazines and Small Presses Are Set Up

Who runs literary magazines and small presses? Who pays for them? And how does the way they are organized influence their publishing decisions?

Every literary magazine and press has a different answer to these questions. That said, publications often fall into one of a few possible categories based on size, staff, and funding. Below I've given sketches of the major types of publications that could be reading your work. This list is not exhaustive. Instead, it is meant to show the range of editors and motivations behind literary magazines and small presses.

Online magazine with one or two editors. With a little time and website-building knowledge, one or two people can easily start their own literary magazine, create an email address for submissions, and open up shop. Magazines like this, especially small-scale poetry journals, often publish issues on their own, irregular schedule. They take submissions by email and select writing that emerges from their own writing communities or fits with their personal taste. Small lit mags like these are not usually prestigious in a mainstream sense, but they are often exquisite and beautifully curated.

Student-run literary magazine at an MFA program. Another common model blooms out of student interest in publishing at creative writing MFA programs. Journals associated with MFAs generally receive a little funding from their college or university but are mainly upheld by the labor of graduate students in creative writing. These students staff the journal to gain editorial experience and understand the inner workings of a literary magazine. Editorships change regularly, since MFA students graduate in two or three years. Issues come out on a regular schedule, often twice a year. Sometimes the issues are in print, accompanied by regularly updated online content; sometimes the journal is published entirely online.

Professionally staffed literary journal at a college or university. Another type of literary magazine, which is more likely to think of itself as a "journal," is affiliated with a college or university and run by a paid staff. Because this level of reliable funding is rare, magazines like these are often prestigious and publish print issues as frequently as quarterly, with a strong subscriber base and solid pay for published pieces. MFA students and unpaid staff may work as readers, but the editors are paid for their work. The journal is financially dependent on the university they are associated with, which usually ensures their longevity, except when a university administrator changes their mind about funding it.

Long-standing, independent print literary magazine. Other high-quality literary magazines function without the support of a college or university. These magazines feature a medium to large masthead and may publish regular print issues while also publishing actively online. The most prestigious, moneyed magazines pay editors for their work. They may function as a nonprofit and receive funds through subscriptions, advertising, or online classes associated with the publication. Other independent magazines, which are likely less prestigious, are a volunteer-run effort with a few bucks here and there to pay for printing or submission manager fees.

Chapbook micropress. The smallest of small presses often has roots in a DIY aesthetic and is run by one or two editors. The editor(s) hold occasional open reading periods and publish hand-stitched chapbooks when they have the time, generally selling the chapbooks only through their website and at in-person literary gatherings. After selling out of the initial print run of fifty or a hundred copies, they may make the PDF available digitally for free. The editors may publish their own writing through the press alongside that of the writers whose work they've accepted.

Shoestring small press with a following. This type of small press has a strong reputation among a specific community of readers, even if its books don't typically receive mainstream coverage. Run on volunteer labor or with a few partially paid staff, it has carved out its corner of the literary world and become a reliable source of compelling new writing. Its books are typically perfect-bound (glued, not stitched) and have strong production value. They might be distributed by a small distributor like Asterism.

Small press with a big impact. Some small presses, even though they're run by a staff of two or three, manage to break into the mainstream. Though they might publish as few as two books a year, their books are reviewed in major venues, featured on punchy year-end lists, and shared widely by readers. These presses know how to focus their time and attention not only on production but also on promotion. Many of their readers might not even know they're reading a book from a small press, while other readers go to this press regularly for risk-taking but accessible writing.

Midsize press. Some small presses are actually quite big, employing a number of people and treating their press as a business. They still prioritize values over profit — many are run as 501(c)(3)s — but they believe that long-term financial sustainability requires cultivating a wide readership. They may also receive literary grants and corporate donations. These presses may have started as one- or two-person publishing outfits and grown over the years into their current iterations. Midsize presses can be understood as a category of publisher all its own — smaller than the Big 5 houses and independent from the publishing conglomerates but still operating mostly according to the procedures of Big 5 publishing.

• • •

Small presses and literary magazines differ not only on the basis of size and funding but also on the basis of time. Some publications crop up and close within five years (or much less). Others run for decades. Some literary journals suddenly shut down, simply because the college that supports them decided to cut their funding. With smaller publications, a website may just stop being updated, and without formally announcing it, an editor moves on with their life. Other times a major masthead change takes place, and the publication's quality shifts dramatically. Because publishing is such a shoestring business, it can be hard to guess where a publication will be in a few years.

When you submit, therefore, you're not just submitting to a particular venue but to a particular venue at a particular time. Becoming familiar with a publication's trajectory should factor into your decisions about where to submit. Ask yourself: Is this small press solid enough that they will keep my book in print long-term? Is this literary magazine doing right by its legacy, or is it resting on its laurels? Will I feel good about this publishing decision five years from now? Where do I fit in this publication's story?

How Your Submission Will Be Read

The process of evaluating submissions looks relatively similar across most publications, even though who is doing the work might be different. There are roughly four parts to the process: receiving the submission, first reads, further evaluation and decision-making, and responding to the submission. These stages are more distinct at larger publications, where each of these tasks is assigned to a different member of the staff. They blend together at smaller publications, where editors often perform all these tasks at once.

If you've just sent your submission, my hope is that this section will set your mind at ease by making the process of evaluating submissions more transparent. For your next submission, you can then tailor your strategy to the real-life process behind the scenes.

Receiving the Submission

The first step of a publication's reading process is the longest, and it has the least to do with the outcome of your submission. Once you press Submit (or put your submission in the mail), your submission joins the queue of pieces waiting to be read.

On Submittable, editors see this queue as a long line of titles extending to the bottom of the page. For mail submissions, a physical stack of manila envelopes grows by the day. It can be overwhelming for an editor to confront all this unread work, although it can also be exciting to imagine the gems that wait there.

The period of time your piece sits in this queue will vary based on the publication. At prestigious venues that receive thousands of submissions, yours might wait six to nine months before anyone even looks at it. The timing of your wait could be affected by the academic year or publishing schedule of the venue you're submitting to as well. Many university-affiliated literary journals, for example, do not read submissions in the summer.

Submitting at the beginning of a reading period sometimes gets you a quicker read, since it places your writing at the top of the queue for that period. Other times, however, editors may wait to respond to all submissions at the same time, or they may hold your piece for longer because they are discussing it in more detail.

Try not to worry about indications that your submission is being read. On Submittable, you'll see a Received icon next to each submission you've sent. When this icon changes to In-Progress, it can be tempting to assume that editors are now reading your piece. But In-Progress can mean almost anything. An editor might simply have assigned the submission to a first reader, whose inbox it will sit in for months before they have a chance to look at it. Don't put too much stock in Submittable's labels.

Instead, put your energy into working on your writing. Readers and editors will get to your submission when they get to it.

First Reads

With very small publications, the process of reading a submission might be relatively simple: The editor of the magazine or press reads each submission. They pare submissions down to a short list they will read again. After another read or two, they decide what they want to publish, perhaps in conversation with the other editor, if there is one. That's the end of the consideration process. Because there are only a few people (or a single person) at the helm, they don't have to build in multiple stages of deliberation.

With medium-sized and larger publications, the reading dynamics become more complicated. That's why I have included two stages of evaluating submissions: first reads, followed by further evaluation and decision-making. These two stages differ because many publications divide their staff into distinct roles known as readers, who do first reads, and genre editors, who make the final decisions. These positions might be known by different names, even though they denote the same role at a publication. Types of editors other than readers and genre editors also play important roles, including managing editors, who manage operations, and editors in chief, who give the last word on major decisions about the publication and may do a final read of submissions. But it is readers and genre editors who are most directly involved in selecting which submissions to publish.

Readers evaluate your writing first. Their job is to select the most promising submissions to pass along to editors. Readers are likely committed writers, but they may have less experience and fewer accomplishments than the editors of the publication where they read. At a university-funded journal, for example, readers might be first-year MFA students, while the editors are second-year MFA students, MFA graduates, or professors. Other publications take applications for readers, posting calls on social media when they need help evaluating submissions. These readers may ultimately become editors, if they stick with the publication and contribute reliably to the decision-making process.

Readers are responsible for reading every submission in the queue, which often amounts to hundreds of pieces of writing split between however many readers there are for that genre. They likely read in batches, spending a few minutes with each submission until they decide on their vote. With some publications, a no vote means the publication immediately sends you a rejection letter. A yes or maybe sends the submission to an editor for closer consideration. With other publications, more safeguards are in place: two readers might read each piece, declining only those that receive two no votes and moving split votes to the maybe pile. With still other publications, editors might look at every submission, taking into account readers' votes before making a final decision.

The reader's taste, along with the specificity of a venue's needs, clearly affect this moment in the consideration process. One reader might love your writing while another shrugs at it. If you get the first reader, your piece gets passed along to an editor; if you get the second, you receive a rejection.

There's no set amount of time that a reader will spend with your writing either. At some point in your writing life, you have probably received advice to make the first page of your piece (or first lines of your poem) unputdownable, and this is solid advice. Every reader wants to have a reason to keep reading from the very beginning, especially when they are in the position of evaluating so many pages in a sitting. Your goal during this stage of the submission process is for your writing to immediately display its importance (the stakes of the writing) as well as its competence (the style of the writing).

With your opening lines, convince readers that your piece is worth reading in full. Then take them on a journey they will want to share with the editors.

Further Evaluation and Decision-Making

If you've made it to this round, your writing is now being considered more seriously. At a smaller publication, this may simply mean the editor rereads pieces they initially liked and makes a final decision on them. At a larger publication, the editors read the submissions recommended to them by the readers. These editors are usually divided by genre: poetry editor(s), nonfiction editor(s), and fiction editor(s).

Editors are likely to read your piece closely and in full, since it has already been vetted by the readers. If there's only one genre editor, they may make decisions on their own and send out acceptance and rejection letters accordingly. If there are multiple editors for a genre, they may meet and discuss which pieces to accept. Editors may have to run their choices by the editor in chief. Or everyone on the masthead may meet once per publication cycle to put together an issue that coheres by theme. Acceptance letters often obscure the lengthiness of this process and the discussion behind editorial decisions. Acceptances are often as brief as "We loved your piece and would like to publish it."

Encouraging rejections emerge from this stage as well. If your writing makes it to the genre editor, but they do not ultimately accept it for publication, you typically receive a rejection that lets you know you were close. Some encouraging rejections even say, "Our readers were particularly impressed by this work." Much of the writing that reaches this stage is publishable, and whether or not it gets published is a judgment call.

For literary magazines and small presses using the contest model, a guest judge usually selects the winner from a handful of finalists, which have been chosen by the readers and editors of the publication. As mentioned in chapter 5, editors sometimes offer publication to nonwinning submissions of a contest. In these cases, more editorial deliberation takes place after a formal winner is selected.

Responding to the Submission

Once the decision to accept or decline is made, the editors send a decision letter to the submitting writer. Most publications send rejections as soon as they know they won't publish a piece, which means rejections arrive more quickly than acceptances. Editors don't like rejecting your hard work. It's a necessary but difficult part of the job of publishing new writing.

Acceptance letters often take longer, as do positive rejections, since the process of deliberating and decision-making takes time. A long wait is sometimes (but not always) a sign that your writing is advancing further in the evaluation process.

When you receive an acceptance, the letter will likely praise your piece (briefly), ask you whether it's still available, and offer to publish it.

If you've reached this stage, congratulations! Now you can turn to chapter 8 and read about all that takes place after acceptance.

The Unofficial Story

That's the official story, at least. The *un*official story — the real way publications find themselves pulled together — is less cut-and-dried than the stages outlined above. A well-designed literary magazine or a book with your name on it can be beguiling, making you forget about the hard work and messiness that went into it.

Literary publications are often flying by the seat of their pants, just like the rest of us. Perhaps some literary gatekeepers operate from a row of well-lit, uncluttered desks with jazz playing in the background. But most of them do not. They are as scrappy, determined, and last-minute as many writers. They're under-resourced, determined romantics who make time in a busy life to do what they love.

In most cases, the people who run literary magazines and

small presses are writers themselves. They might be at similar career stages to the submitters they are reading. Though some editors are relatively established, such as MFA professors and people who make money from their publishing positions, it always feels like a struggle to get paid, supported, and recognized for the literary work you are doing. Literary gatekeeping, at least when it comes to small presses and literary magazines, isn't usually enforced by people who are deeply comfortable in their roles.

The following sketch might be more accurate. When I was a reader for the nationally known literary magazine at my PhD program, my days were irregular and frantic. My one tether, every morning, was to sit in a chair and write for an hour while I ate my oatmeal. Then all bets were off. Sometimes I attended class, then went to the library to do my weekly reading while the sun went down. Sometimes I worked a shift in the on-campus writing center. Sometimes I had to write a paper, collaborate with a classmate, or do a logistical task for our literary magazine like sending out copies to subscribers. The work was ever-changing, and my days were both inspiring and exhausting.

Every night I would return home to my basement apartment, where three tiny windows looked out on a patch of mulch. Sometimes I was too tired to do anything more than boil noodles for dinner. But sometimes I felt the hum of unfinished business. Those nights, I knew it was time to read submissions. Sitting on the old couch my landlord had left in the apartment, I opened up Submittable. I began with the oldest submissions in the queue. I read at least a page of each submission as closely as I could. If the submission was obviously not right for us, I would skim until I knew for sure. Most submissions weren't right for us, because the writer wasn't familiar with the taste of our journal.

Every tenth submission or so, I would come upon a submission that felt like it was part of a shared conversation. Pieces like these were practiced and consistently engaging. They were also off-kilter enough to fit our innovative sensibility. I would read those submissions closely, crossing my fingers that the writer would land the ending.

After I had read each piece, I voted on the submission. With a yes or a maybe, I added a short note explaining my vote and reaction to the piece. No answers were usually obvious enough not to explain, and frequent enough that it would have been a burden to write a note for each one. I voted maybe more often than yes. A maybe vote meant a piece felt promising but didn't quite deliver on its potential. It led to a second look by the genre editor, and most likely a positive rejection. Yes meant I felt certain the piece had to be in the magazine. I knew it was a yes when I lost myself in it. I forgot I was reading submissions.

But I *was* reading submissions. And it all happened on an old couch in the basement apartment where I lived in Denver, my feet up on my landlord's coffee table, streetlights shining through my tiny windows. My bowl from dinner sat empty at my feet. I would read submissions for exactly an hour, after which I gave myself permission to start my bedtime routine. I did this several nights a week. I could get through twenty submissions in an hour. There were hundreds of submissions in the queue.

The editorial staff did meet from time to time. We had an office in the English department that four or five people could squeeze into. Next to it was another, bigger office that was filled with decades of copies of the magazine. Our meetings weren't about deciding on submissions, which all happened on Submittable. Instead we discussed our varying roles and the needs of the journal, focused on logistics that had to be taken care of, and tried to figure out who was going to take over editorship the next year.

Eventually I took over as prose editor. This meant I made the final decisions on fiction and nonfiction submissions after readers decided on their votes. The editor in chief approved these decisions, but I decided what got published. It was hard to believe. I had submitted to publications like this for years, and now I was in charge of what got published.

Yet my editorial power did not feel quite so personal. Rather than passing down decisions from above, the submissions themselves determined my decisions about what to publish. So did the aesthetic our magazine had established over decades of regular issues. The submissions I accepted were so clearly on our wavelength that choosing them was simply a matter of acknowledging that.

I waffled occasionally. Some pieces had a wonderful concept, style, and beginning but faltered at the end. Others were stylistically fascinating, but it was hard to tell what the stakes were. Still others were resonant in their content, but the writing didn't feel practiced on a sentence level. I was rooting for every piece I read. I *wanted* to find the stakes, the style that clicked into place, the ending that brought it all together. I often said to myself, "I wish they had given it one more draft!"

Evaluating submissions taught me the value of a phrase I had long reviled: "This wasn't the right fit for us." I had seen this phrase in rejection letters for years, and the sentiment always rang a little hollow. As an editor, however, I understood that my editorial decisions had less to do with the writing itself and more to do with the journal. There was no such thing as an objectively good piece of writing for us. The journal's taste was quite specific. I began to understand successful writing not as an isolated achievement but as a deep engagement with our literary context.

The "best" writing doesn't work because of its unarguable merit, that is. Instead, it meets readers where they are. Its awareness of its audience emanates from every word and phrase.

Who are you writing to? Who are you writing for? These questions will guide your writing out of an exclusive focus on "quality" and toward a more connective stance. This is good for your writing and, I believe, good for your submitting. Someone's going to read what you've written. How do you speak to them?

Writing Prompt

Let's visualize the audience of your writing. Write your response to the following questions as a short character sketch.

Describe your ideal reader: Who are they? What is their life like? Where do they live? What do they do for work? Who are their favorite writers?

Now imagine them reading your writing. Where are they sitting when they read it? What is their reaction? How do they feel? Who would you like them to share your writing with?

Later, when they think back on your piece, what would you like them to remember? What do you want them to get out of your writing?

Understanding your audience is especially helpful in the revision process, when you have to make hard decisions about where to cut and what to add. If you have a reader (or editor) in mind, those decisions will be easier. Writing becomes more about making your work right for a certain reader than pursuing the ideal of perfection.

Connecting with the right reader really does happen. When the right piece meets the right person, a light flicks on. We are all working hard to find a moment when the page suddenly illuminates. What can you do to give that moment to editors? How can you light up their day, their hour, with writing that feels as if it were written especially for them?

7

Three Case Studies

You're not the only one submitting your writing. Behind every published poem, story, essay, and book is an author working hard to achieve their publication goals. All writers, with very few exceptions, have thrown themselves into some version of the work described in this book. The writing you see in the world is almost always the culmination of a long and circuitous journey to publication.

This chapter gives you strength for that journey by telling the story of three different small press writers' paths to publication. Their stories include years of writing, plenty of rejections and, finally, the thrill of publication. They also show the importance of creating a sustainable writing and submitting practice. That's because the most important thing you can do as a writer seeking publication is to teach yourself how to keep going, no matter the circumstances. These writers stayed with it, believing in their writing until it found a home — first when they began to receive acceptances from literary magazines, and then when their books were published with small presses.

These writers' experiences aren't meant to be representative or all-encompassing. Instead, they provide three of many possible paths for how to approach your work as a submitting writer. Each approach has its own merits. Every writer's publication story is built out of their own values and daily practices.

Your job, of course, will be to build your own story. What resonates for you in the following stories? Where do you see yourself? What's the next step on *your* path, and how can you envision following it to (and beyond) publication?

Lisbeth White

I first met Lisbeth White just after her poetry collection *American Sycamore* was published by Perugia Press, a small press in western Massachusetts. My class had read two of her incredibly wise lyric essays, and I asked her to visit us. She led us in a meditative writing session where we dug into the roots of our connection with the earth. Her guidance, like her writing, was grounded and generous. It opened up our writing.

Lisbeth brings a unique combination of healing energy, lush imagery, and precise attention to all her writing. I interviewed her about submitting in part to understand how she brings that generous attention to her submission practice. She spoke with me from her home in Port Townsend, Washington.

Lisbeth's writing journey began when she was a teenager. Her auntie, who was a poet, introduced her to poetry, and writing soon grew to be a bridge for Lisbeth, a connection with the rest of the world. Lisbeth majored in creative writing in college. When she graduated, she wanted a job that connected with her poetry. She earned her master's in psychology and became an expressive arts therapist.

All along she was writing. For years she wrote for herself.

Then, almost suddenly, the writing began to seem more purposeful: "At some point, I was writing some poems, and I had this feeling about them." Lisbeth said to herself, "I think this might be a collection. I think this is a project." She realized she needed help bringing her poems into the world.

She didn't want to go through the process of getting an MFA, since she already had a master's. Instead she found a different place where writers gathered, shared work with each other, and talked about writing: writing workshops and craft-focused conferences. The first she attended was VONA (Voices of Our Nations Arts Foundation), a multigenre workshop for BIPOC writers. Attending VONA felt like a moment of arrival: "This is it! These are people who are writing? I love these people. I want to be a part of this." Lisbeth went on to attend numerous writing workshops and conferences, including Callaloo, Tin House, Writing By Writers, Corporeal Writing, Bread Loaf Environmental Writers' Conference, and Blue Mountain Center.

It was during these workshops that Lisbeth found herself surrounded by writers submitting their work. At first she wasn't entirely comfortable with the idea of submitting. But she wanted to push herself toward that uncomfortable edge, both to challenge herself and to expand her sense of audience. These dual goals lived alongside each other: "I do have a part of me that is very achievement oriented," Lisbeth says. "And, underneath that, I am also very much thinking about putting work out in the world as building my community."

When Lisbeth began to send out her writing, she received a few early acceptances from online literary magazines. The editors of these relatively small magazines gave her direct feedback on her writing. As a writer just beginning to submit, Lisbeth valued their individualized attention. These acceptances gave her energy to keep going. She began to submit to larger, more prestigious literary magazines. But she didn't have as strong a sense of that landscape, and the results didn't turn out as well.

This was how she learned to prioritize her writing goals when seeking publication. “I like the experience of submitting to smaller places better,” says Lisbeth. “As much as I want the prestige and have that side of me that really is ambitious and wants to achieve, I also have to think about my own morale as a writer, and what feels good, and what helps me to keep writing.” What helped her to keep writing, she found, was to work closely with editors and have them engage thoughtfully with her work.

Lisbeth also learned to tailor her submissions to literary journals that felt right for the specific piece she was writing. After she finished and began to submit her poetry collection (more on that in a moment), she began to write essays. She took a few creative nonfiction classes to support her work in the genre. Then she submitted her essays to publications that shared an ecological, environmental standpoint. Since the essays were rooted in a connection to the earth, they fit with the publications.

In the meantime, Lisbeth was submitting her full-length poetry manuscript, *American Sycamore*. After publishing most of the poems in literary magazines, she sent the book out consistently for a year. She received around thirty rejections, including some positive notes from editors. But she was discouraged by the response. “Do I need to rewrite this? Why isn’t it landing?” she asked herself. She took a break from the process, letting the manuscript sit for six months.

Finally, a friend encouraged her to send it out again. She sent it to a few presses, testing the waters again. One of them was Perugia Press. The previous year, they had sent her an encouraging note on her submission: “We really love this,” they said. “We think it’s going to find a home. If it hasn’t, feel free to send it again.”

Lisbeth was in Paris when she received the acceptance from Perugia Press. The editor left a voicemail on Lisbeth's phone, which she only checked after a two-week hiatus from her American SIM card. How did it feel to receive an acceptance for her first book? "I felt a little bit like, 'What, is this happening?' And then I felt so happy that she called. It felt like this was the thing I had been waiting for." The voice-to-voice contact and the editor's generous words about her book meant so much. The acceptance also felt a little surreal. "Even though I wanted it, I don't know that I was actually expecting it."

Not only was the book accepted, but Perugia Press felt like the perfect press for the book. Since 1997 Perugia Press has been publishing a single book each year, always first or second books by women. Because of their singular focus, they were able to give a level of attention to *American Sycamore* that few presses can provide. "I always joke that working with Perugia and a small press have probably ruined me, because it set the bar really high in terms of the experience I had as a first-time author."

Lisbeth had about a month to soak in the acceptance. Then she and the editor leaped into revisions. Lisbeth was also included in the process of production and design, which included incorporating the artwork of Lisbeth's friend for the cover. When the book came out, Perugia supported a virtual launch as well as a trip to Massachusetts to promote the book. Since Lisbeth didn't have built-in networks from an MFA, she found that the press opened doors and made important connections for sharing the book.

Meanwhile, Lisbeth found herself working on another book-length project, even though it wasn't a book from the beginning. Lisbeth had put together a panel for the &NOW Festival with two other poets who used witchy, ritual practices when writing. At a reprise of the panel at AWP, it just so happened that a North Atlantic Books editor was in attendance. The editor reached out: "Have you thought about doing a book around this?" The panelists assembled a proposal to submit to the press, and the proposal was accepted.

The book, *Poetry as Spellcasting: Poems, Essays, and Prompts for Manifesting Liberation and Reclaiming Power*, was their "pandemic project," as Lisbeth puts it. She and her fellow editors met every week for a year and a half. The book was fundamentally collaborative, bringing together work from kindred poets and writers into a necessary salve for the times. "It was hard, but it was also very sustaining," says Lisbeth. *Poetry as Spellcasting* was published six months after *American Sycamore*.

These publishing experiences, Lisbeth says, have yielded multiple benefits to her as a writer. For one, they have enabled her to find creative community beyond her existing networks. Sharing her work has also opened up her writing: "I'm still this creative person who still wants to generate and still needs creative aspirations for myself," she says. Having books in the world has provided opportunities, connections, and newly open doors that allow her to keep writing with visibility and accountability.

Lisbeth still feels like a newbie, she says, but if she had one piece of advice to share, she would advise writers to submit and publish in accordance with their deepest priorities. "Let yourself learn what kind of experience you want to have with your writing," she says. "The goal is for you to keep writing. If you find yourself in a place where you're not feeling good about yourself or your writing, none of the publications matter. Really let yourself discover what feels good and what feeds back into your writing. And then focus your submissions along that channel as long as it feels good."

Jackson Bliss

I first learned of Jackson Bliss's writing during an epic year in which his first three books were published: a short story collection, a novel, and a memoir. His social media campaigns, interviews, and online presence made those books hard to ignore. When I read his story collection, which was published by one of my favorite small presses, I was lit up by Jackson's expansive, sensitive prose, as well as the way he represented characters from a variety of racial backgrounds, including mixed-race and nisei writers like himself, with thoughtfulness and a deep attention to context.

When I interviewed Jackson, he had recently returned to Los Angeles after a short stint in Ohio. He led me through his journey as a submitter, beginning with his very first attempts at sending out his work.

Even before he began seriously submitting, Jackson says, "I think I did what every aspiring writer does at least a couple of times, which is launch a firework into the ocean and then get sad that no one can see it." He sent several of his earliest stories to *The New Yorker*. He knows now they had almost no chance of publication. Still, he says, submitting something in the beginning gave him a sense of artistic accountability — the idea that someday, someone would read what he wrote.

It was only later, during his MFA program, that Jackson started submitting in earnest. He built a "fanatical" organizational system with two stacks of index cards, one alphabetized by literary magazine name and the other by the name of the piece he submitted. It was helpful to be so organized, Jackson says. "It was also just heartbreaking because everything was rejected." That said, the rejections provided information. When a piece was rejected twenty or twenty-five times, he knew it was time to revise again. His goal was to send up to a hundred submissions a year.

"Like everyone else in my program," Jackson says, "I craved being read. I craved finding my readership. I craved having my work out there. I wanted to have work that meant something to someone so that someday they'd see my name, and they'd say, 'Oh yeah, Jackson Bliss!'" Eventually — on his birthday — Jackson's first short story was accepted. He'd been submitting for about eight months. From there he stayed with his submissions process. He always tiered his submissions, starting with his most preferred journals and following up with more accessible venues. He received between one and eight acceptances a year. Some years were slower. Some were a windfall.

In the meantime, his organizational system migrated onto the computer. Jackson enumerated each submission, gave a star rating based on how positive the response letter was, and even issued himself an acceptance percentage at the end of each year. He also devoted his time to reading literary magazines. Understanding the communities where he was submitting his writing, he says, was a bedrock of his education as an emerging writer.

Eventually Jackson finished an early version of his novel and began submitting it. He tried literary agents first, both those who had reached out to him because of his short stories and those he queried directly. But Bliss's writing is conceptual, formally transgressive, and difficult to categorize. It can't easily be compared with other Big 5 writers, which is important in providing "comps" for an agented book, and is more language driven than much literary fiction. Agents said they couldn't sell the book.

Jackson began to realize that publication with the Big 5

houses wasn't the right path for his current writing: "I started feeling like, 'I need to take an inventory of my own reality here.' It doesn't seem like the New York publishing industry is really into my voice, my aesthetics, into my particular narrative modality." He knew small presses, on the other hand, have always been willing to take risks with the writing they publish. As Jackson reflected, "I should go to the part of publishing that will probably be most open to my writing and that has championed other writers that I really respect." One example was Karen Tei Yamashita, whose *I Hotel* was published by Coffee House Press and ended up a finalist for the National Book Award. "*That* should be my inspiration."

By now all three of Jackson's books were finished. He started submitting them to small presses. At first he focused on the biggest houses, including presses that could be considered midsize, which work with both agented and unagented writers. He had several close calls. He even met with editors who closely considered the book, but this never quite led to publication. He tailored his books to specific submissions calls, expanding his notion of where his books might belong.

Then, almost a decade after he began submitting early versions of his books, he got the news he had been waiting for.

First Jackson heard back about his novel manuscript, *Amnesia of June Bugs*, from 7.13 Books. The editor had read the book and loved it but had a rule that less than 50 percent of the books he published each year could be by men. The coming year's catalog no longer had room for the book. Jackson asked very delicately, "Could you push it to the next season's catalog?" The editor said yes.

Soon afterward *Dream Pop Origami*, an experimental memoir, was accepted by Unsolicited Press. A friend of

Jackson's had recently announced their own book deal with Unsolicited, and Jackson liked the look of the press. He submitted his memoir. The editors wrote back with an acceptance just four days after he sent it.

Finally, *Counterfactual Love Stories*, his short story collection, won the Noemi Book Prize in Fiction. "I couldn't believe it," Jackson says, "because I never win prizes. And they're incredibly hard to win." He was in conversation with another press about the book at the time, but he ultimately decided to publish with Noemi because he knew they would connect to the right readership for the book.

These three acceptances were a major windfall, especially after years of submission, rejection, and ongoing revision. "I've got to say," Jackson says, "this easily could have gone the opposite way. There are a number of times I've thought about giving up. I just happen to be incredibly stubborn." He'd read enough books that he believed there was space in literature for his writing. He stuck it out. He stayed with the process.

That's the only difference, Jackson says, between writers who get published and those who don't: endurance. As he learned during his internship with a New York publishing house, "Waiting ten, twenty, thirty years to publish your first book is totally normal. The problem is, in the beginning, we're all obsessed with the fairy tale."

Once Jackson found publishing houses for his work, working with editors on his books helped break him out of his creative habits and see the work anew. A good editor, he says, is friends with the manuscript first, and the author second. At the same time, Jackson felt there was always respect for him as an artist. The editors' feedback was insightful and detailed, but they understood that ultimately each book was his book.

When it came to releasing his books, Jackson did much of the promotion himself. Knowing the budgetary and staff limitations of small presses, he taught himself video editing, Instagram stories, and other platforms that would help promote his books. The presses contributed to promotion in their own ways. One press created a full website for the memoir that mimics the book itself. Another used its influence in the literary landscape to draw attention to the book, including through their annual prizes. The third entered his book in literary festivals and postpublication contests.

"I put everything I could into it," says Jackson of the year when his three books were published. At the end of a year of book launches, he was exhausted. He admits he has trepidation about engaging in such a busy year of publication and self-promotion again. But there's also something nourishing, he says, about sharing his books on his own terms, in partnership with the small presses that believe in them. His writing is out there now. Knowing this, he can approach publishing exactly how he wants to.

Jackson advises writers at the beginning of the submission process to appreciate publication's role in your writing journey. The writer-editor relationship, Jackson says, is an important opportunity to develop your voice. So is sharing your work with an audience: "You get to show the rest of the world that you have art out there, and you become artistically accountable in a tiny way to a growing readership who starts to slowly figure out who you are." In fact, you begin to figure out who *you* are as a writer through the act of sharing your work. "Your audience forms a crucial dialectical relationship with your writing," Jackson says, "and that's going to be true from a literary magazine all the way until the end."

Zoe Tuck

I first met Zoe Tuck at a bookstore in the next town over from mine, where I was invited to be part of a local poetry reading. Zoe was another of the readers, and from the way she interacted with the other writers it was immediately clear how interconnected she was with the Northampton poetry scene. Especially because I was a writer new to the area, I was impressed by her engagement with the living fabric of writing community.

When I read her writing, I discovered it was generous, funny, quietly deep, community minded, and *fun*. Reading Zoe's poetry feels like being in the room with a friend who is always willing to get real about life.

On a cold fall day, I met Zoe at her favorite coffee shop in Northampton. Over herbal tea, she told me about her trajectory as a published poet and writer.

Zoe's writing origin story took place in high school, when she attended a poetry class at the local community arts center in Austin. She met two local poets there, who she came to admire not just as poets but as active members of the poetry community. These poets taught classes at local spaces and out of their living room; they held a regular reading series; they published a folded and stapled journal called *Skanky Possum* that featured work from local writers. This was what a poet's life looked like, as Zoe understood it then. She soon fell in with the two poets and apprenticed herself to them.

A few years later, Zoe moved to the San Francisco Bay Area. She began to connect with the Bay Area poetry community through local reading series, and she also started a reading series with a friend. Her first publication bloomed from this community. Two local poets had been publishing *Try!*, a folded and stapled lit mag with only fifty to a hundred copies of each issue. You could only get the issues by being at readings and having one handed to you by the editors. "It was just there," Zoe says. "It seemed like the gazette of Bay Area poetry at the time." Zoe submitted her poetry to *Try!* Her poems came out in the next issue.

Meanwhile, Zoe continued to invest herself in the literary landscape. She worked at Small Press Distribution (closed now, sadly), which helped her become familiar with the expansiveness of the small press ecosystem, including publishers beyond her own geographic community. During Occupy Oakland, she published another piece of writing in the anthology *A List of Our Demands*. Together, in the spirit of the movement, the editors and contributors hand-stitched the anthology in the editor's living room.

Zoe also got involved with Timeless, Infinite Light, an upstart small press in the Bay Area. After she submitted a short story to an anthology they were assembling, Zoe was invited to join a reading celebrating the book at the Sutro Baths. In this roving reading, writers were stationed at various points in the ruins, and the crowd was encouraged to move among them. Zoe wore a toga. At the end of the reading, everyone sent wax paper boats with tea lights into the ocean.

Zoe's relationship with Timeless, Infinite Light grew. "As has been the template for me," she says, "after befriending them and sending work to them, I started to work with them." She became an editor and did promotional work for the press. Then the other editors asked to publish a book of hers. It was her first book: *Terror Matrix*. Timeless, Infinite Light published it four years after her poems first appeared in *Try!*

Around the same time, Zoe had another important publication: her poems appeared in *Troubling the Line: Trans and*

Genderqueer Poetry and Poetics, a groundbreaking anthology that was the first of its kind. When the anthology came out alongside the publication of her first book, she felt like, "OK, I'm here. I've arrived."

For Zoe, arrival meant that the pressure of wanting to be involved cooled down. She had a new sense of herself: "I feel like I'm part of things, so I can turn my attention back to the work." She left the Bay Area and arrived in western Massachusetts. She grew more disciplined and less precious about her writing. She built up an accumulation of work.

Over the years, Zoe told me, this accumulation led to several finished manuscripts. Some of these were published as chapbooks in the intervening years by publishers like DoubleCross Press and Daisy Mayhem Press, which produce fine handmade limited editions. Other poetry accumulated into full-length collections. So when an editor at BUNNY, an imprint of Fonograf Editions, reached out to Zoe, she had two books at the ready. BUNNY accepted *Bedroom Vowel* and published it. It was Zoe's second full-length book.

This is when I had to stop her. "Hang on," I said. "You published this book without ever submitting it? They just asked you for a manuscript, and that was it?"

Zoe admitted that yes, that was how the book was published.

"And this happened for both your books?"

Zoe laughed. This was exactly how it had happened.

This is not to say, Zoe reminded me, that she had never spent time on Submittable. For a while she submitted her books to the major contests and the prestigious magazines. She fixated on the idea of a big, prizewinning book. But in the end, Zoe said, this publication strategy didn't work for her. "Pretty much everything in my writing life has come from one kind of relationship or another," Zoe says. "Working with people at a press, teaching, editing." She decided to stick with the publication process that worked for her.

These days, if she does aim for publication, she is drawn to venues that publish writers she considers herself to be in conversation with. A literary journal is not just a literary journal, Zoe says. "It's a room I want to be in." When she enters that room — when her writing is published — it is an act of sharing, of communication. "I want to give my gift," Zoe says. "I made it, I carried it, and someone else cared about it, and now I can give it."

Zoe admits her approach might not be for everyone. "I am such a raging extrovert," she says. But even for the introverted, it is possible to engage, communicate, and contribute. "You have to do some kind of literary service, and kind of suspend your desire for a transactional outcome," says Zoe. It's not a quid pro quo. "But you have to participate in it." For her part, Zoe now teaches classes through Threshold Academy, the nonprofit educational space that serves as a base for her community activities. She hosts the But Also reading series out of her own house. She is also a member of the Belladonna* publishing collective.

Zoe's advice for writers is twofold: "Find your people" and "Start something." You could start an online literary magazine with no overhead, aside from website fees. You could host a reading series at your house. Do anything that feels doable to you, because starting something will accelerate your journey of finding your community. People in this community may eventually publish you or ask you to read in *their* reading series. More importantly, they'll become your friends. Community is not about getting published — it's about being with the people who give meaning to your life.

Writing Prompt

Tell your own story of publication,
as you imagine it ten years from now.

Where do you imagine you will be in your writing life in ten years?

What will you look back on and appreciate, even if you don't appreciate it now?

How do you want your publication story to be told?

After you have imagined this story, ask yourself what you can do in the present to make it come true. How do you live the publication story that feels right to you?

Publication rarely acts as a hand from the clouds that sweeps you up to fame and fortune. Instead, it is a deeply contingent, involved process in which you build your own relationship to the practice of sharing your work. Yet the three writers whose stories are told above share an essential quality: a combination of perseverance and patience. They simply kept writing and submitting, even when they weren't getting lots of validation for their work.

These writers also share a deep inhabitation of process. It can be tempting to focus on the goal of publication itself, which is likely what drew us to submitting in the first place. But these writers live in the process rather than the outcome. Lisbeth prizes the editorial feedback and community that come with publication, not the achievement itself. Jackson marks milestones that are independent of the eventuality of acceptance; he gamifies his submissions, for example, by noting acceptance percentages at the end of each year. Zoe sustains herself on relationships, not publications. By the time each of these writers sees their writing in print, the publication itself isn't the point. They've already managed to build a sustainable system for living in the process before publication arrives.

What does it mean for you to build a sustainable process? How can you take joy in the present, even while writing, submitting, and imagining the future? Before you end this chapter, take a few minutes to reflect on how you can make a home in your unique process.

8

After Acceptance

Behind every minute of your submitting journey is the dream of acceptance. It's what we long for, what we tap our fingers waiting for as we refresh our email for the thousandth time. It's what makes us jump out of our seats when we get the news. It's the light at the end of the tunnel, the moment when all our hard work bears fruit.

When you receive an acceptance, celebrate! Tell the nearest person, even if they're a stranger in a coffee shop. Tell the people you love. Take a minute to note the acceptance in your files (see chapter 3) and withdraw your submission from any venue that is still considering it. Then order pizza for dinner and have a massive slice. Crack open a tiny bottle of champagne. Breathe freely with the knowledge that your hard work is being recognized and that you've achieved a major goal.

Now take a deep breath. The publication process isn't over yet.

Plenty will be required of you after acceptance — more waiting, likely more revising, and more contact with the editors. This chapter lays out those important steps so you know what to look for between acceptance and publication.

As you enter this new phase of your relationship with writing, where you'll work *with* literary magazines and small presses instead of submitting *to* them, remind yourself of your goals from chapter 1. These will allow you to stay focused on what you want out of publication. Then engage in the below steps with all the attention and care that you've always given to your writing. Stay with it, just as you've stayed with submitting. Seeing your work published is just around the corner!

The Steps after Acceptance

Contracts

After acceptance, most small presses and literary magazines will send you a contract to sign. One exception to this practice is small DIY outfits that forgo contracts in favor of handshake agreements. Some literary magazines may ask you to respond in the affirmative to an email that states the rights you grant by agreeing to publish your piece with them. The rest will ask you to sign on the dotted line.

While contracts can be stressful, they are useful protections for writers. They're a way of guaranteeing a publication's obligation to you, making sure that they are as committed to publishing your work as you are to publishing it with them. Contracts formalize the agreement so that if anything goes awry, you have somewhere to turn.

That said, we're writers, not lawyers or agents. Contractual language is nothing like creative writing, which means it's confusing for many of us. So what are you supposed to do when you receive a contract you're expected to sign? (In this section, please remember I am not a lawyer and this is not legal advice.)

When it comes to literary magazines, contracts are on the simpler side. They'll often ask for "First North American serial rights," which means they get to publish your piece for the first time in North America in a serial publication. The rights usually revert to you a short time after publication, so you can publish your piece again in a larger collection (or republish it in another periodical, if the second periodical accepts previously published writing). In addition, venues often ask for acknowledgment of their publication in any future collections that include the work. Sometimes contracts will request the exclusive right to publish a work for a period of time after publication, which means you can only republish the work after that time period. If your shorter submission is part of a book that may be published soon, it's good to pay attention to this part of a contract.

In general, you will likely sign literary magazine contracts as is. If you are working with a particularly complicated contract or piece of writing, however, you may want to get another eye on it through the Authors Guild, mentioned below.

Book contracts are more complicated than literary magazine contracts. Every press requests different rights. What you should know, first of all, is that you don't have to sign their contract as is. You can negotiate toward a more advantageous setup for you as an author. You may ask to keep translation rights, for example, or the right to license the work to formats like film. You may request a different type of copyright, such as a Creative Commons license. You may negotiate on the delivery date of the manuscript or the timing of publication. It can be difficult to have these conversations with a publisher if you don't have representation, since contract language is so specific. Still, if aspects of the contract particularly stick out to you, it's worth bringing them up with your press.

If you're without an agent and would like professional advice, the Authors Guild provides advice to members who are negotiating contracts. Alternatively, you can hire a literary lawyer. If you don't have major concerns but want to understand better what you are agreeing to, you can also request a meeting with your editor to go over the contract. Publishers have power in this situation, but you, as a writer, have power, too.

Some people would advise you never to publish your writing without a contract. This advice makes sense in most situations; your writing is your writing, and you have every right to insist on protecting yourself. At the same time, I think it's reasonable to consider the context if you are offered publication without a contract.

As I've described throughout this book, literary publications differ in their levels of professionalism and access to funds. A tiny online literary magazine with no budget and no paid staff is generally in no position to be drafting contracts, negotiating, and filing paperwork for every writer they publish.

Personally, I think it's fine to publish with very small literary magazines that don't have the structure, staff, or expertise for a contract. Even chapbook publishers, if they're hand-printing copies in their basement, aren't necessarily doing a disservice to authors they publish without a formalized agreement. If you agree to publish your writing without a contract, just know that you're investing your trust in the publication and that you have elected, on the basis of that trust, to go without guarantees of how your writing will be published.

When you're publishing a full-length book, however, I would insist on a contract. You need assurance that there will be consequences if the press doesn't fulfill their commitment to you. This kind of professional interaction can sometimes feel at odds with the community spirit behind many small presses. But the truth is that community works best when publications respect their writers, including financially. Always ask the difficult questions about formalities surrounding publication, if questions remain.

Editing

After revising for months or years, I always long for the moment when I can wash my hands of a piece of writing and call it done. Acceptance, alas, is not that moment.

Occasionally, a literary magazine will publish your writing without suggesting edits. But most literary magazines and all small presses insist on at least one round of edits before your writing is published. Many go through multiple rounds. Working closely with writers on their pieces is a big part of editors' jobs, and receiving this kind of attention is a real benefit for you as a writer. Editors' detailed feedback almost always helps make your writing the best version of itself.

There are several stages to the editorial process, depending on the time an editor has to spend on your work. At a small literary magazine, you might just receive a few line edits that help land the ending or clarify a point of confusion. Shorter pieces of writing, like poems, are also likely to require few edits. If you are publishing a longer piece of prose, especially at a well-resourced literary magazine, you may receive substantial edits on the language, content, and even structure of the piece. Whole sections might change or be cut.

After a round or two of edits, you will likely receive copyedits as well. These ensure the piece adheres to the literary magazine's style guidelines and that facts are correct, place names are accurate, and your grammar and spelling are on point. At smaller literary magazines, developmental editing and copyediting may be folded into one step.

The editorial process is especially robust when a small

press is publishing your book. You will likely go through several rounds of edits, in a Google or Word document you share back and forth, until both you and your editor are satisfied. This process can take months. You may be asked to focus on structure, sentences, and flow as well as larger questions about theme, stakes, and narrative arc. You may find yourself changing your book more than you thought possible when you originally submitted it.

That's why the editing stage can be a difficult process. You've already put your book through the wringer on your own, and the last thing you want to think about is one more character who isn't working, one more poem you need to revise, or one more section that needs to be rearranged to make the narrative arc of your memoir work.

Remember two things as you dive into edits: First, you don't have to make changes you don't want to make. If an editor suggests something that doesn't fit your vision of your book, push back respectfully. Explain your reasons. Hold firm if you need to, while also seeking to understand the editor's point of view.

Second, this round of editing will almost certainly make your book better. After you glance through each round of edits, take a few days to process. Even if the edits frustrate you or seem at odds with your intentions, you may begin to realize that many of them are helpful. You'll acknowledge important problems with the manuscript you half knew were there but needed someone to point out. Let the edits motivate you to make the changes you need to make, even if they aren't the exact changes suggested by the editor.

It's worth checking in about a magazine or press's editorial process before you sign your contract, if you want to make sure your manuscript gets the attention it needs. As with everything in the small press world, editorial processes vary widely. The main thing is to know what you are signing up for.

Production

Production refers to everything that comes *after* you deliver your completed, edited, final manuscript and *before* a finished copy of the issue or book arrives in the world. This is when the editors and designers of the publication make your writing into a readable, accessible physical or digital object.

The production phase concerns writers very little, but you will be asked to contribute at a few important moments. Early on you will need to provide a third-person author bio for the contributor notes or author page. You can use the same bio as the one you used in your cover letter, or you can tailor it to the length and vibe (brief, casual, or professional) of the publication itself. Be brief, clear, and nonexhaustive. Two to three sentences is enough.

Later, you will be asked to approve proofs, which is your chance to make sure the layout of your writing matches your intent. Was everything transferred from your original document to the printed page? Things to check include spacing and indentations, italics and bold, alternative formatting like block quotes, and visual elements. This is the final detail to make sure that your writing will look the way you want when it is published. Writers are often asked to read through the text a final time, too, in order to catch any last-minute errors.

If you are publishing a book, you may be invited to give input on the cover design. Editors sometimes ask for a list of book covers — like a mood board — to guide their design process. They may ask whether you have a cover image you'd like to use. Even before you have a book contract, keep an ongoing list of your favorite book covers and images so you have something on hand when these questions come up. Not every press will say yes to your requests, but if you have opinions, don't be afraid to share them. It's your book. Your press should take your opinions into account.

In the production phase, aim for a balance between being clear about your needs and allowing production editors to do their job. Book designers, like editors, are working hard on behalf of your writing. Be grateful but firm about your design preferences, especially when reviewing mock-ups of the cover or internal design. Request another option if you need to. Don't be afraid to respectfully speak up.

Printing and distribution follow on the heels of final decisions about page or book design. Printing books and literary magazines takes time, and it takes even longer for copies to reach bookstores and online booksellers. Be patient with these aspects of the production process, since you won't be cooling your heels for long. Soon after production, if not during it, you will begin to promote your book or the literary magazine that's published your writing.

Promotion

Many writers are less than thrilled about the idea of selling our writing. Even if you are comfortable with self-promotion, spreading the word about your publications can feel quite distant from the act of writing itself.

That's why I try to think of promotion as an *extension* of writing rather than as something that comes after the writing is finished. Readings, interviews, reviews, and interactions with readers are ways of continuing to revise the meaning of your writing, even after its publication. Try to retain the creative spirit that inspired your writing in the first place. How do you bring that spirit to the events and conversations surrounding publication?

Practically speaking, promotion can run the gamut from a few posts on social media to a yearlong campaign. If you're publishing in a literary magazine, your promotional efforts might be relatively simple. You can post about the publication on social media, add a link to your website, and if you have the chance, read the piece publicly while crediting the magazine. Since you are being published alongside a number of other writers, you can also read and share your fellow contributors' work. Promotion for short-form publications is a unique opportunity to share both your own and others' writing at the same time.

If you are publishing a book, promoting it may be a long and multifaceted journey. Most small presses will send you a marketing questionnaire well before your release date. Every press's marketing sheet varies, but they all have the important job of helping the publisher (and you) promote your book. The sheet might ask for comparable books or authors, sales points or excerpts, institutions you're affiliated with, and audiences you imagine for the book. They'll also ask you about your previous publications, reading series, book review venues, book reviewers, and booksellers that might be interested in holding an event or providing coverage, as well as awards for which you'd like to submit the published book. These questionnaires can be overwhelming if you are starting from zero. It's a good idea to keep a running list of this information so you don't have to do all your research in one go.

You'll also be responsible for soliciting blurbs, the quotes that appear on the back (and sometimes front) cover in which established writers praise the book. Presses sometimes help contact blurbers the writer isn't already in touch with. When you request blurbs, make sure to be gracious, thoughtful, and accommodating of your prospective blurbers' time constraints and busy lives. Many established authors receive far more blurb requests than they can reasonably provide. At the same time, don't feel bad about asking. Blurbs are part of publishing, whether we like it or not, and the writers you'll ask know that. Keep writing for long enough, and you'll have the opportunity to provide blurbs yourself.

Many people will tell you that publishing with small presses means doing much of your book promotion yourself. This is true, although it is increasingly the case for Big 5 houses as well. With tight publishing margins and a social media landscape dependent on the author's public image, all publishers rely on the active participation of writers to get the word out about their writing. That said, large presses employ publicists and marketing professionals whose sole job is to get books on the national map. Small presses excel at selling books to their established community, but they rely on writers to promote their work more widely.

Despite having fewer resources for promotion, small press books regularly win big awards, make it onto highly visible end-of-the-year lists, and achieve widespread recognition. This is in part because small presses have the flexibility and vision to publish groundbreaking work, as discussed in chapter 1. Especially in poetry, where innovation is the norm, small presses regularly receive National Book Award and Pulitzer Prize nods. Fiction and nonfiction published by small presses (and, increasingly, university presses) achieve national attention as well. You can't guarantee this kind of reception, but you can work hard alongside your publisher to spread the word about your book.

You can also hire your own publicist, if you have the money. This is an expensive but time-tested way to receive increased coverage for your book. Be warned: hiring a publicist will cost at least several thousand dollars, and often tens of thousands. If you decide to supplement your promotional efforts with a freelance publicist, make sure to get in touch with them six months to a year before your publication date.

Becoming an *author* — rather than simply a writer — can be a strange and difficult transition. Here are some things you can do to keep your book promotion active and community focused while honoring the writing spaces that have sustained you:

- Keep an ongoing list of friends and contacts in the literary world. Reach out to them on publication day to let them know about your book.
- Stay in touch with the editors and publications who have published your writing.
- Reach out to reading series in your local area. Set up readings with authors you know or admire in cities where you can travel.
- Set up podcast interviews with your favorite literary podcasts.
- Write a craft essay to share your practice with fellow writers.
- Write a list essay highlighting books that have inspired your writing, focused on a subject area that is important to your book.
- Conduct an interview where you and a fellow writer ask each other about your books (or, if someone is willing, ask them to interview you).

- Contact people you know who teach, and offer to send them a desk copy of your book.

Social media is also an unarguable engine for book sales and interest. Being active online can sell books. In general, the more you post, the more engagement you get and the more likely you are to be on readers' maps. But social media can also take you away from your writing or be a cause for anxiety, which simply isn't worth it. If you aren't on social media, or if you aren't good at social media, don't worry. Do as much social media as feels generative to you, then get back to writing.

Regardless of how you choose to promote your writing, you can think of promotion as an act of community. You have been influenced, inspired, and shaped by the writing that precedes you. Now is your chance to add to that conversation and enliven it.

That's why the moment of sharing your writing can also be a moment of gratitude. It's likely that a whole bunch of people supported your journey toward publication. Publication day is a good time to thank those people! I try to devote a significant amount of my promotion time to reaching out to those who have supported my writing, especially those who helped me with the specific piece being published.

If you've just placed a piece in a literary magazine, is there a friend or mentor who provided indispensable guidance? Send them a physical copy in the mail with a note of thanks. If you're publishing a book, you'll likely have written an entire acknowledgments section. Consider reaching out to each person in the acknowledgments. Write physical thank-you notes. Allow yourself the time to reflect on everything — and everyone — that brought you and your writing to this moment.

Getting Back to Work

Suddenly, it's publication day! Miraculously, the literary magazine you've been published in goes live online. Your box of books arrives in the mail. You click the link. You tear open the package. There they are: your words firmly in print. It's real! You've been published!

You share the good news. You celebrate.

You take a breath.

Whew. What's next?

For many of us, that moment is when another piece of writing begins to hover on the horizon. You may decide to write another book. You may want to play with shorter pieces for a while. You might want to take a well-deserved rest.

Regardless of what you do after publication, your writing will always be there. It may not be today, it may not be tomorrow, but you can always return to the page when you need to. This is the lesson to remember when publication day is upon you: as great as publication is, the page is where everything begins.

9

The Vulnerable Work of Sharing Your Writing

How we talk about submitting is essential. That's why, in this book, I've returned over and over to a few main aspects of submitting: Community and connection. Staying true to your goals. Most of all, I've asked you to think about submitting as a practice that gives back to your writing. Talking about submitting in these ways, I believe, helps us build the literary community we want to inhabit.

But there's one last word we need to consider when we talk about submitting. That's the word at the heart of it: *submit.*

Many writers are hesitant about using *submit* as a term for sending out our writing. For those of us who are sensitive to language, the word *submit* can imply a power imbalance. It can connote surrender to a superior force. It might bring to mind a mighty gatekeeper who stands at the gate of literary accomplishment, striking down all those who don't pass muster. Before that gatekeeper, the humble writer begs for acceptance.

When you submit, you hand over your work and wait for a decision to be passed down from above. That's what it can feel like, at least, when you've just written something and sent it to editors to consider for publication.

But we do not have to think of submitting this way. It was a student in my original "How to Submit" class who suggested we focus on a different definition of the word. As my student reminded us, we don't have to use the warlike meaning of the word. Instead, we can submit in the sense of "giving an offering."

You can *offer* your submission, my student suggested, to editors, to other writers, and to readers. You can give it as a gift.

Submitting in this spirit is an act of connection and community. It is also an act of faith: we submit our writing without knowing what the response will be. We believe in it, but we don't know who else will. That's what makes your submission a gift.

Believe in what you're giving. The rest is up to those who receive it. Eventually, like any offering, your writing will end up where it belongs.

When Your Offering Comes Back Around

Years ago I was giving one of my first official readings. I had been invited by a friend to join a reading series where I'd seen some of my favorite writers share their work. Now *I* stood in front of the three-panel painting of the last supper rendered in molasses, ready to read. I wore dark jeans, a half-zip sweater, and glasses. I tried to seem accomplished. An audience of thirty people sat gathered in front of me. Among them were writers I respected, friends I knew, and strangers I didn't.

I read an essay about having inflammatory bowel disease called "The Last Remedy." It described, in clipped syllables, how every time I ate my stomach clenched and roiled, how I walked through life with my disease brewing inside me, affecting everything I did. What I wrote about wasn't beautiful, but I tried to write about it in a beautiful way. I listed the remedies I had tried to fight off the illness. I charted the slow and steady process whereby my belief in those remedies wore off and I was left on my own. I had to figure out who I was without a remedy. I had to make a home in my disease.

When I finished reading, the audience clapped. Some members of the audience even came up to me. They recognized themselves in the essay, they said, because they had bowel problems, too, or because they had a chronic illness, or because their loved one did. Those who knew me said they felt like they understood me now. Those who didn't know me introduced themselves. They told me the essay had meant something to them.

I never expected this. A year earlier, I had written the essay in the dark of my basement apartment without knowing what it would become. I submitted the essay just a few days after I finished it. To my surprise, it was accepted just a few days later. Within a month, it was published.

When "The Last Remedy" was published, it opened me up to a community I hadn't known I was longing for. Other chronically ill and disabled writers shared the essay on social media. They got in touch and shared their information. I connected with other writers who had IBD. I read the literature of chronic illness, finding a sense of home I'd never known I was looking for. There was a deep intimacy in our shared understanding. We knew what it felt like to live in a body that did not cooperate with us.

By the time I gave my reading from "The Last Remedy," I was starting to come home to myself. I was a person with chronic illness, I realized, a person who wasn't afraid to talk about shit, who was writing the uncomfortable facts of a disease most people didn't like to talk about. Now I could share myself in front of a real audience: I was giving an offering. The audience really listened to me, and the offering circled back.

Publishing that essay changed my writing. It changed how I thought of myself. The offering of my words in print, for others to read and hear, all started when I took a chance on my story by submitting it.

When it was accepted and published, an alchemical reaction took place. I realized my story was bigger than me. I finally understand how to follow my story where it led.

The Little Things

But publishing our writing is not just about the big moments. It's also about the little interactions and relationships that add up over a writing life. These instants of magic and connection can be just as buoying as the life-changing acceptance.

After "The Last Remedy" was published, I began to write more about IBD. A few of those essays were accepted, and I had the chance to work with editors on reenvisioning and publishing them. But there was one essay I spent years writing and revising. I weathered years of rejections for it. I could never quite get it right. Finally, it was accepted at a beautifully designed, well-known literary magazine.

Soon after acceptance, the copyeditor sent me her edits, which were as keen and thorough as I had ever seen. She pointed out my variations in usage, asked questions about formatting, and gently brought up grammar mistakes. Her comments were sensitive and thoughtful. Responding to them was a small but electric joy. It meant a lot to me how deeply she engaged with what I had written.

There was one particularly thorny question in the comments. It pitted my intentions as a writer against the publication's style guidelines, which left a gap we had to navigate with nuance and sensitivity. We went back and forth in comments in the margins. She shared helpful suggestions. I thought aloud about the problem. For a brief moment, we were wonderfully immersed in the inherent problem of language. Even though we were just going back and forth in a Word document, I felt like we were having a real conversation.

It was a beautiful moment to inhabit. Here were two people both working as hard as we could to find the right words. We approached the dilemma with a clear passion for writing and reading, even as the right words evaded us. We nerded out about language and talked sincerely about the significance of the craft decision. We appreciated the hum of questions that are beautiful because of their very tininess.

At the end of the day, this is why we write: We care *so much* about our stories. We spend hours, days, years finding the words we need. Then, in the magic of publication, we meet others who care as much about words as we do. This is a deeply affirming experience. It changes us, and it can change everyone who encounters it.

• • •

The vulnerable thing about submitting is, you never know exactly how or when your writing will find these connections. What if your writing is rejected? What if these stories of community and connection are hard to come by? What if your writing doesn't receive the same amount of generosity and thoughtfulness as you've put into it?

These are valid worries. Sharing what you love is absolutely a risk. It can take a long time to achieve your publication goals. People's responses to your writing can never be predicted. Even with this book to accompany you, it's impossible to account for every aspect of the submissions process.

I'd like to invite you, for a moment, to welcome this uncertainty. In the following prompt, I'll ask you to reflect on your fears, worries, and struggles when it comes to submitting.

Writing Prompt

Reflect on the feelings that reading this book has brought up for you, especially regarding the vulnerable work of submitting.

What are your worries, fears, or unresolved questions about the process of submitting your writing? What are you unsure of? What parts of the process are difficult to understand and contain?

List all the things you're unsure of or worried about. Get them out of your mind and onto the page.

When you've completed this prompt, I would like you to do two things. First, put the prompt in front of you and read what you've written. Acknowledge what you're feeling. Accept it. Allow yourself these unknowns.

Then close your eyes. Envision yourself in a room that is

only for writing — a place you may never have even seen before. Let this be a place where you see yourself writing in five years, ten years, or further in the future. It's a place where you have everything you need. This is your writing room.

Once you've gotten comfortable, open the door. Let the worries, fears, and questions from your prompt into the room.

Designate a spot for these feelings next to you on your writing desk. Acknowledge them. Give them a little space. Then return to your writing.

Ask yourself: What does it feel like to let these tensions into a place where the writing can thrive? What does your writing have to say about these tensions? What feelings and thoughts arise?

Stay at your desk as long as you need to. When you are finished, leave everything where it is and leave the room.

Now open your eyes. Jot down any wisdom that came to you.

As you do this, remember that writing will always be there for you. As you go deeper into your journey of submitting and publishing, your writing can always help you answer the tough questions and show you the way through.

• • •

If your writing is one form of inherent wisdom that can act as a guide for your submissions, another is the people around you. You're surrounded by friends, family members, and fellow writers who care about your writing journey. What happens when you bring your worries, fears, and questions to them? What wisdom will they share?

There are many ways to structure this kind of support for your submission practice. One is to talk with writer friends and ask them about their relationship to submitting. You could set aside a time each month to submit your writing together, in person or virtually. These meetings could also include work that's adjacent to submitting: building your social media presence, researching literary magazines and small presses, writing a strong cover letter, and getting involved with literary publications. You could finish each session by celebrating the work you got done and talking about your goals for next time.

In addition to writers you already know, you can seek out online and in-person groups organized around submitting. Women Who Submit, which welcomes women and nonbinary writers, grew out of a submission party of six writers gathered around a kitchen table and now has chapters in twenty-three states. They hold virtual and in-person submission parties and share resources around submissions. Submission parties may also be held by writing workshops in your city. Local writing workshops often have one-day and multiweek classes on submitting, querying, and writing book proposals, which provide additional structure and feedback on your submission materials.

Many of the venues discussed in chapter 2 also feature resources that connect writers who are submitting their writing. Poets & Writers, for example, publishes regular print issues and online articles about writing and publishing. Their website features a directory of writing groups. Chill Subs publishes regular columns about submitting and hosts online classes about writing and submitting. For more resources like these, see appendix B.

Most importantly, don't be afraid to talk about submitting! Publishing is the complicated, unwieldy, but essential system that determines readers' ability to access our work. If we don't talk about it, the big questions will haunt us, drawing a divide between the initiated and uninitiated. Instead of keeping the path to publication a mysterious process, we can share the ins and outs with others who are working toward related goals.

The writing world has begun to embrace this conversation in recent years. Writers talk openly about their publishing deals on social media, and growing attention to the stories behind publication highlights small presses and literary magazines. Many MFA programs are now including more professional development, which includes information on publishing in a variety of venues. Submission resources are increasingly springing up, spearheaded by writers who wish to help others like themselves.

We have begun to recognize that our writing is not separate from how it is published. It's up to us to continue this trend by talking to each other about submitting. There is power in sharing our experiences of seeking publication. If we are to find a home in the process of sharing our work, we have to help build that home.

This means being honest about the difficulty of submitting, too. It means sharing our successes as well as our failures. It means supporting the publications we submit to and doing what we can to help our fellow writers. Finally, it means sharing our knowledge and skills once we've gained them. When we discuss submitting openly and with generosity, this tangled process begins to bind us together.

Stay True to Yourself

Last of all, I want you to remember that what happens on your submissions journey does not define you. You are a unique and important writer, regardless of publication. You bring something to the world that has never been seen before.

I know it can be hard to stay in touch with that vitality when you're submitting. Rejections can feel like judgments — and rejections always outnumber acceptances. Even acceptances don't feel like the ultimate validation, since you have readers' opinions to worry about next, and then how much money you make from your writing, and after that, editors' opinions about your next writing project. It can be hard to feel like you've ever truly arrived.

If you feel discouraged, return to your goals. Remind yourself that publication is a means to an end, not an end in itself. Ask yourself: Why am I submitting? How does publication fit into the larger picture of my writing? How can publication help me meet my goals?

Those questions are secondary, however, to how you feel about your writing on its own. Ask, Am I staying true to myself? Do I believe in my writing? Am I being honest, authentic, and unafraid in my writing practice?

If the answer to those three questions is yes, don't let a few rejection letters deter you. Editors have specific tastes, flaws, and distractions. Limitations of time, money, and circumstance have a lot to do with whether a piece gets published as well. Beautiful, necessary pieces of writing often fly under the radar, especially when they are doing something that hasn't been done before. If an editor doesn't see what you're doing with your writing, that's OK. Your writing is your writing. Nobody else's.

What matters is that you are writing exactly what you need to write. You are giving your unique gift to the world. If you keep developing your voice — if you keep searching for the story you need to tell — you will find it. If you keep searching for the editors and publications that click with your writing, you will find them, too.

In the meantime, make a home in the act of putting your words on paper. Make a home, too, in the literary world, where you already belong simply by virtue of the fact that you write. Allow submitting to motivate you, give energy to you, inspire you. Let it fill up your writing.

The greatest achievement — far beyond publication but also a precursor to it — is to regularly show up for yourself and the writing you believe in. Stay with it. Remember the connection that will come with sharing your work. This sense of connection is a place we can arrive every day, when we put words on the page.

APPENDIX A

Frequently Asked Questions

Many questions arise in the process of submitting, especially when entering this landscape for the first time. As always, I recommend you talk about your process with fellow writers or trusted people in your life. Bouncing concerns off others is the tried-and-true way of working through questions about submitting.

Below I share my own responses to some of the most common questions about submitting. These are my opinions, to be taken with a grain of salt. *Your* answers matter most when it comes to your writing.

How long will it take me to get published?

Everyone's publication journey is different. Timing, practice, and luck play into the picture, but so does the type of publication you are aiming for. If you want to, you could likely get published a few weeks from today. This would mean choosing to submit to a literary magazine with a very high acceptance rate and a very fast response time. It would probably mean sending them your most polished work.

Alternatively, it could take years or even decades to see your writing in print. This is more likely if you submit exclusively to high-prestige publications. It takes time to find your voice fully and exquisitely, in a way that is recognizable at an extremely competitive venue. When your writing is ready, you'll also have to wait for the right piece to end up at the right publication, not to mention the lengthy response time of many competitive publications. The odds are tough for even the most impressive writing.

Waiting a few weeks and waiting a decade aren't the only two options, of course. My point is that the ball is partially in your court. How long it takes you to get published depends on where you are in your writing life and the publications you're shooting for. It also depends, to a great extent, on luck. This last factor is outside your control, but never underestimate the strange turns of fortune that influence decisions about publication.

Stay true to your goals through all of it. If you believe in those goals and work toward them authentically, a decade or more won't seem like a long time. Similarly, a few weeks might seem like just long enough.

How important is prestige? Should I only publish with the "right" presses or magazines?

The answer I want to give to this question is, "Who cares about prestige? You can't measure art in a hierarchical way. Art is its own thing, independent of our pecking orders and best-of lists." I really believe this, at least on a theoretical level. What we gain by ranking our writing is far smaller than what we lose.

That said, prestige is a thing in the world that everyone has to negotiate with. That's why it makes the most sense to ask this question on a practical level: Will prestige help you reach your writing goals?

For some of us, the answer is yes. If your goal is to make money, share your writing with a wide audience, or receive extensive editorial and marketing support for your writing, pursuing prestige is not a bad idea. Better-funded publications will be able to provide these things, and prestige usually correlates with better funding.

If your goals are to feel admired and receive validation, on the other hand, I would caution you against using prestige to fulfill those goals. Many of us want someone to tell us we're good enough. But no amount of success will ever be enough to convince you that you are worthwhile. There will always be someone more successful, always a laurel you haven't yet won. Prestige is an engine for anxiety if you're relying on it for your self-worth. Consider how you might find a sense of validation through your work without relying on external standards of success and achievement.

If your goal is to get your work out there, to give yourself an end point for your writing, or to subvert the status quo, prestige may not be what you're looking for. That's terrific. Don't let mainstream attention to certain venues and certain types of publication get to you. Submit to the publications that give you what you need.

What should I do while I'm waiting for a response?

Obsessively check Submittable, refreshing every ten minutes until the status of your submission changes! Just kidding. On anxious days, that's exactly what I do.

But if you want to be healthier about it, I would suggest compartmentalizing your anxiety by preselecting a specific date and time to obsess about submissions. For example, give yourself an hour every month when you'll check Submittable, submit more if needed, meet deadlines that are coming soon, and stress as much as you need to. Then close all your tabs, and don't think about submitting again until the next month.

In the meantime, immerse yourself so fully in writing that you forget all the other stuff. When you need to, take time to intentionally rest.

How fair is the process of submitting and publishing writing?

Publishing is not fair, at least not in the ways many of us expect it to be. There are *some* mutually agreed-on guidelines: publications running contests, for example, usually abide by the CLMP Contest Code of Ethics.

In general, however, taste is subjective. It's hard to know what *fair* would mean in a field so defined by differing aesthetics and values. This lack of objectivity is part of what makes the writing world so dynamic and beautiful.

Will an exceptional piece of writing always receive the attention it deserves? No. Will hard work and commitment to writing always result in the exact publication you are aiming for? Probably not. You never know how your writing is going to mix with the editors who read your submission, the historical circumstances you find yourself in, and the readers who ultimately hold your writing in their hands.

All this said, there are rules I believe you can rely on: In general, people who keep writing and submitting for a long time (I'm talking decades) achieve something they can define as success in publishing their writing. In general, getting involved with literary community makes it easier to find a home for your writing. In general, the more you write and submit, the more you will publish.

If you do these things, you will have a good chance at

getting what you need from submitting and publishing. You may not walk the exact road you envisioned when you first started writing, but the road you walk will become yours. That's as fair as it gets.

Can I make money writing?

Yes, eventually, if you explicitly work toward that goal for years with never-flagging business savvy. But don't expect making money as a writer to mean sitting down every day, writing what you want, and getting paid for it. A significant amount of writing-related income actually comes from gigs such as teaching, freelance editing, and speaking engagements. Other income can come from writing freelance nonfiction (such as opinion articles and criticism). It is extremely rare for a person to make enough money from only their fiction, creative nonfiction, or poetry to live off. To get to that point, no matter how talented you are, requires you to win a major award or write a book that becomes a runaway bestseller. These things happen, but they're not something you can plan for.

Be aware that trying to make a living from writing may dampen aspects of writing that drew you to it in the first place. You'll have to write on assignment, for example, or tailor your projects to publishers' needs. You may find that thinking about writing all the time, or doing writing-adjacent work, saps your creative energy. Making money as a writer can change your relationship to writing.

If you don't make your living from writing, you're in good company! Working a nonwriting job is very common among published writers.

I recommend choosing the path that allows your writing to thrive. If deadlines, pitches, and assignments from editors fuel you, as well as teaching and speaking regularly, it's not unreasonable to aim to make a living from your writing. If you can get the creative space you need while working a non-writing job, that's a good thing for your writing, especially if you don't mind the job itself.

How many literary magazine publications should I have before publishing a book?

Some writers have no publications at all before their first book is accepted. Some have a few short publications they gained on the way to finishing their book. Some have four or five high-prestige publications. Some have published in twenty or thirty literary magazines.

The answer to this question, therefore, varies based on a couple of criteria. For one, what kind of book are you writing? My own books have often been composed of smaller parts (poems, stories, and essays) that can easily be published separately from the full manuscript, which led to a number of short publications before my first book appeared. Many novelists and writers of book-length nonfiction, on the other hand, don't have short pieces that can easily appear on their own. This means they publish less often in literary magazines, since they are concentrating their writerly attention on their full-length books (although some literary magazines do publish excerpts from novels).

Your own validation structure also plays into this question. Does aiming for literary magazine publications fuel your writing? Or is working on shorter pieces a distraction from working on your book? How important to you is building connections with writers and editors through literary magazine publications? Do you read literary magazines? Are they inspiring to you? If you *like* writing short pieces and submitting to literary magazines, it's worth the time. If you don't — if you're just doing it for the publication credit — you can let yourself off the hook.

From the perspective of editors and agents, you don't have to publish in literary magazines before you publish a book. Literary magazine publications are just like any other qualification: they are an argument in your favor, but what determines whether your book gets published is your book itself. Less prestigious literary magazine publications, especially, are unlikely to move the needle significantly. More prestigious publications can sway editors, but achieving them takes a real commitment to your shorter writing. Very occasionally, editors or agents might encounter your work for the first time in a literary magazine, which could lead to them reaching out to you and inquiring whether you have a book. In this last case, it's not so much the fact that you published in a literary magazine as the quality of your writing itself that leads agents and editors to you.

It's not worth it to stack up literary magazine publications simply in the hopes that they might help you publish a book. Literary magazine publications are important in their own right: They give you the opportunity to share your writing. They help you develop community, give you the benefit of an editorial eye, and allow you to explore the appropriate contexts for your work. If you pursue literary magazine publication, do so for these reasons rather than to bolster the case for your book.

What is it like to become a published writer?

Everyone has their own publication story, so it's hard to make generalizations about what it will feel like to see your work in print.

Personally, one thing I've experienced is a sense of elation when my writing is accepted, followed by a surprising sense of disappointment. It's weird to want something for so long and then to find out that life is pretty much the same on the other side. You get up, make breakfast, go to work. Your screen door whacks you on the butt on the way out the door. The check engine light of the car is still on — you really need to get that looked at. The weather's nice, but you forgot your sunglasses.... You get the idea.

Wanting to be published makes sense. It feels so much better to say you're a writer if you've been published, and sharing your writing is such an important part of the writing process. I found it easier to live with myself once I knew my writing was available to read, speaking the things I had spoken only to myself for so long.

That said, prepare yourself for the day when you *do* get published. How will you make sure your writing is sustainable regardless of the world's pronouncements on it?

Don't idealize publication. Work toward it, yes, even long for it, but don't imagine it will solve all your problems. It will solve one or two of them! Which will be wonderful. But, if you keep writing after you're published, you'll still be facing down blank pages, incomplete plotlines, and ideas that hum but that you don't yet have the words for. Being published won't solve those problems, so it's best to just get started on figuring them out. Focus on feeling good *now*.

Should I ever give up?

Giving up is always possible. That's the magic in writing, in a way: we keep doing it even though we don't have to. At any moment we could throw down our pen (or our laptop). But we don't. We keep trying to find the words.

Inspiration is real. So is the deep desire to communicate, and so is every motivation that brings us to writing. If you still feel connected to that inspiration, to that deep, motivating thing, I don't think you should give up on writing.

Submitting can be discouraging, but it's not personal. Rejection is tough, but it's inevitable. We receive these difficult messages from the world, but if there remains beneath them that desire to write, don't give up.

That said, you can stop anytime if you need to. I won't judge you, and no one else should either. Stopping doesn't mean your life is meaningless. It just means you found your meaning in something other than writing.

How can I build a life in writing?

For me, a life in writing means a few things. One is community: sharing a space with other people who care about writing. When I work alongside others toward deeper articulations of meaning and more textured expressions of the world, I feel a sense of purpose and connection. Any act of language, even reading or writing alone, gives me this feeling. Communication is an act of community.

A life in writing also means tuning in to your most essential work. I have this desire to search, to imagine, to make things. Doing this regularly returns me to myself. It reminds me that I'm not just a body trying to pass through the world unscathed. I'm a creative force. Channeling that energy makes me feel like I'm really living.

Finally, a life in writing means acceptance. Not acceptance

from other people. Acceptance of yourself. The deeper you get into this practice — writing, submitting, publishing — the more you will come to embrace your peculiar gifts. That's the acceptance I really want, at the end of the day: a belief that the thing I do is worth doing. It doesn't have to be perfect. It just has to be what I make it.

Publishing is not incidental to these goals. Instead, submitting your writing is where you encounter yourself. It is where you see the part you play in the big picture: how you fit in, what you have to offer others, and where your writing is at home.

APPENDIX B

Directory of Additional Resources

This book is not the only resource available to you as a writer submitting your work. Below I have listed additional guides to publishing as well as community resources that provide support to writers working toward publication.

Online Guides to Submitting Your Writing

Lincoln Michel's "The Ultimate Guide to Getting Published in a Literary Magazine," published on *BuzzFeed* in 2015, remains a fun and transparent guide to submitting to lit mags from someone who has submitted a lot and has had success doing it.

Tony Tulathimutte's "Pitching and Moaning: A Guide to Submitting Your Writing," published in *Catapult* in 2017, is an irreverent and helpful take on submitting, which has the benefit of including a guide to the pitch letter as well.

Samuel Moss's "Introduction to Submitting your Manuscript to Presses" on the 11:11 Press website is a to-the-point guide for writers from the perspective of a small press editor.

Kim Liao's "Why You Should Aim for 100 Rejections a Year," the viral *Lit Hub* article, has become a shared reference point for many writers who are looking to keep themselves accountable to their submitting practice.

Chill Subs' *Write or Die* magazine is a frequently updated resource that features writing about submissions and the writing life, including articles from "When Can You Call Yourself a Writer?" to "What Really Matters: On the Value of Writing Groups."

Poets & Writers, *Lit Hub*, *Electric Literature*, and other writer-facing magazines feature regular content about working toward publication, although their take is not exclusive to writers submitting to literary magazines and small presses, since their articles often focus on books by agented writers published with the Big 5 houses.

Books about Seeking Publication

There are many books that focus on seeking publication. These books don't talk in detail about submitting to literary magazines or small presses (that's why I wrote this one), but I am sharing them because they are helpful guides to many aspects of the writing life.

Kevin Larimer and Mary Gannon's *The Poets & Writers Complete Guide to Being a Writer: Everything You Need to Know about Craft, Inspiration, Agents, Editors, Publishing, and the Business of Building a Sustainable Writing Career* (Avid Reader, 2020) is a comprehensive guide you can return to throughout your writing life. It features perspectives from writers and publishing professionals across the literary world, giving a well-rounded, multivocal survey of life as a writer from the craft of writing to assembling a career.

Courtney Maum's *Before and after the Book Deal: A Writer's Guide to Finishing, Publishing, Promoting, and Surviving Your First Book* (Catapult, 2020) is a humorous, knowledgeable guide to navigating the writing life and publishing a first book with a major press.

Arielle Eckstut and David Henry Sterry's *The Essential Guide to Getting Your Book Published: How to Write It, Sell It, and Market It... Successfully!* (Workman, 2005) is a practical, extensive guide that examines every possible angle of the book publishing experience.

Jane Friedman's *The Business of Being a Writer* (University of Chicago Press, 2018) is an essential guide for goal-driven writers who wish to monetize their writing lives, moving toward a career in which writing fuels their income.

Betsy Lerner's *The Forest for the Trees: An Editor's Advice to Writers* (Riverhead, 2010) discusses revision and publication from the perspective of an editor at a Big 5 house.

Jeff Herman's Guide to Book Publishers, Editors, and Literary Agents: Who They Are, What They Want, How to Win Them Over (New World Library), regularly updated and now in its 28th edition, includes advice for writers submitting a book, especially a book of commercial nonfiction, alongside an updated compendium of presses and agents to submit to.

Writer's Market (Writer's Digest Books) is the classic, regularly updated guide to nearly every publication where you could submit your writing, including book publishers, a variety of magazines, contests and awards, and literary agents.

Community Writing Workshops

While MFA and PhD programs in creative writing play a significant role in the literary world, an increasing number of writers are finding writing community in nondegree-granting workshops with a wide offering of classes. This book, for example, grew out of a class I taught regularly at GrubStreet, a home for creative writing classes in Boston.

Classes like these are available to anyone who can pay for them, and sometimes financial aid is offered as well. Students come from a broader range of ages and positions in life than creative writing students at colleges, and their experience as writers varies more as well. I have found that students at nonacademic writing workshops are also more likely to talk about the business aspects of being a writer, including publishing.

Most major cities in the United States have local writing workshops where you can take classes in person. Many of these centers also offer regular classes online.

Here are a few of the community writing workshops in major cities in the United States:

- Hugo House in Seattle, WA
- Literary Arts in Portland, OR
- GrubStreet in Boston, MA
- Lighthouse Writers Workshop in Denver, CO
- The Loft Literary Center in Minneapolis, MN
- Gotham Writers Workshop in New York, NY
- Sackett Street Writers Workshop in New York, NY
- The Writer's Center in Bethesda, MD

- StoryStudio in Chicago, IL
- Indiana Writers Center in Indianapolis, IN
- The Writing Salon in San Francisco, CA
- Fine Arts Work Center in Provincetown, MA

This list is far from exhaustive. Even my rural town in Massachusetts is near multiple additional writing workshops that offer regular classes as well as informal community gatherings. Search for classes and workshops that work for you in your own city or town. Additionally, since many of these local writing workshops offer classes online, you can choose from a wide array of workshops, no matter where you live.

If you're looking for online-only creative writing classes, LitReactor and Shipman Agency are two good options, and many more can be found online. Some literary magazines, such as *One Story* and *A Public Space*, also hold regular seminars and classes. Individual writers frequently offer their own classes as well, without organizational overhead.

Writing Organizations and Groups

A number of writing organizations support writers who want to share their work. Some of these are major organizations whose names you have already seen in this book:

- **The Community of Literary Magazines and Presses** (CLMP) features regular calls for submissions and expansive databases of resources, not to mention doing general advocacy work for literary magazines and small presses.
- **Association of Writers & Writing Programs** (AWP) provides a number of submission and career resources,

many of them only for members. It also holds the major annual writing conference, which takes place in a different city each spring.

- **Poets & Writers** has an array of free, easy-to-navigate databases that list submission opportunities, writing groups, and literary locations. They also publish regular articles on building a writing career.

The following literary organizations focus on specific communities of writers. Many of these organizations also hold annual retreats and workshops, provide fellowships, run their own literary magazines, or host annual award series:

- **Lambda Literary** nurtures and advocates for LGBTQ+ writers.
- **Cave Canem** cultivates the artistic and professional growth of Black poets.
- **Kundiman** supports writers and readers of Asian American literature.
- **CantoMundo** cultivates a community of Latinx poets.
- **Asian American Writers' Workshop** (AAWW) is devoted to creating, publishing, developing, and disseminating creative writing by Asian Americans.
- **Radius of Arab American Writers** (RAWI) provides mentoring, community, and support for Arab American writers.
- **Kimbilio** develops, empowers, and sustains fiction writers from the African diaspora.
- **Mizna** centers the creative work of Arab, Southwest Asian, and North African artists.
- **Zoeglossia** is an inclusive community for poets with disabilities.

The above list is only a sample of the most prominent organizations. For a full list of literary organizations that serve writers of color, see Kundiman's list, "Literary Organizations That Serve Writers of Color." For a list of literary organizations by state, see the Loft's Literary Organizations page.

Annual Conferences and Workshops

Annual conferences and workshops bring writers together for a week or a weekend to talk writing, work on their craft, and share pointers on the writing life. Most importantly, these workshops and conferences give you the chance to meet fellow writers and make connections that will creatively sustain you.

The largest conference is AWP, an annual four-day gathering of up to twelve thousand writers that features countless panels on publishing and writing, an expansive book fair with booths from a wide array of literary magazines and small presses, and nightly off-site events hosted by publications and literary organizations. AWP gets a lot of attention, but smaller conferences may enable you to make more authentic connections, leaving you feeling inspired instead of overwhelmed. Writing conferences abound each year, and several are likely within driving distance of where you live. For a less academic feel, you can search for annual book fairs and book festivals near you.

Another type of annual offering is the weeklong (or multiweek) writing workshop, which has a less academic, more craft-focused feel. Some of the best-known annual workshops are Bread Loaf, Sewanee, Tin House, and VONA, but these are only a tiny sample. AWP and Poets & Writers both have databases listing upcoming writing conferences and workshops.

Writing Groups

As mentioned in chapter 4, writing groups are an important community-building tool for many writers as well as an opportunity to share early drafts of your writing. If you have writer friends already, you can invite them to a regular meetup where you share excerpts of works in progress, discuss your writing process, and talk about next steps for sharing your work. If you want to join an existing community, both Poets & Writers and AWP have listings of active writing groups that are open to new members.

You can also host a submission party, in which writers set aside a time to get together and send out their writing. Sharing space and intention with other writers who are submitting will help you hold yourself accountable, as well as providing the opportunity to compare notes and share resources.

• • •

However you find them, support and community are essential tools for keeping you engaged in the process of submitting. When you feel worn out from working toward publication, take a class, join a writing group, or schedule a visit to a conference, workshop, or book festival. Taking the leap will both give you energy to keep submitting your work and give you a sense of shared purpose with your fellow writers.

Acknowledgments

Thank you, Reiko Davis, for believing in this project from the beginning. This book wouldn't be a book without your guidance, confidence, and inspiration.

Thank you to everyone at New World Library, especially Jason Gardner, Kristen Cashman, Monique Muhlenkamp, and Tracy Cunningham. It's a beautiful thing to work on *How to Submit* with a press that started by publishing hand-stapled booklets out of a kitchen in the late 1970s. Thank you also to Alan and Ian at *the*BookDesigners for your contributions to the design and to Mimi Kusch for copyediting.

Thank you, Janice Lee, for accepting me, believing in me, and giving me the opportunity to do work I didn't even realize I needed to do. You are a guiding light and a powerful friend, and I am grateful for you.

Thank you to every small press and literary magazine editor I was in touch with at *Entropy* for sharing your sense of literary community and expanding my own. Thank you to everyone at *Entropy* for welcoming me in.

Thank you, Justin Greene, for carrying the torch of the "Where to Submit" list. Thank you to everyone who used the "Where to Submit" list over the years, who taught me so much about literary community and publishing.

Thank you to my students in the "How to Submit" class at GrubStreet for sharing your goals and dreams. You helped me understand how important it was for this book to inspire while also acting as a practical guide. Our brief communities inspired me.

Thank you, Bin Ramke, Laird Hunt, and my fellow editors at *Denver Quarterly*. Thank you, duncan b. barlow and McCormick Templeman of Astrophil Press. Working with you to publish new writing was a wonder for me.

Thank you, Sara Attia, Steven Huang, Neviah Waldron, and Sarah Wu, for thinking through small presses with me at Amherst College and imagining what it means to create a resource that prioritizes small press publishing.

Thank you, Lisbeth White, Jackson Bliss, and Zoe Tuck, for sharing your stories.

Thank you, Keith Scribner, Marjorie Sandor, Jennifer Richter, Selah Saterstrom, Brian Kitely, and Laird Hunt, for your mentorship, advice, and support over the years.

Thank you to my family for supporting my writing at every stage. Thank you, Thirii and Waiyan Soe, for being my home.

Index

About the Author

Dennis James Sweeney is a small press author whose writing spans fiction, nonfiction, poetry, and cross-genre work. His publications include books with Autumn House Press, Essay Press, Ricochet Editions, and Stillhouse Press, as well as short stories, essays, and poems in literary magazines such as *Ecotone*, *The Southern Review*, *Witness*, and *The New York Times*. He has an MFA from Oregon State University and a PhD from the University of Denver. Originally from Cincinnati, he lives in Amherst, Massachusetts, where he teaches at Amherst College.

DennisJamesSweeney.com

NEW WORLD LIBRARY is dedicated to publishing books and other media that inspire and challenge us to improve the quality of our lives and the world.

We are a socially and environmentally aware company. We recognize that we have an ethical responsibility to our readers, our authors, our staff members, and our planet.

We serve our readers by creating the finest publications possible on personal growth, creativity, spirituality, wellness, and other areas of emerging importance. We serve our authors by working with them to produce and promote quality books that reach a wide audience. We serve New World Library employees with generous benefits, significant profit sharing, and constant encouragement to pursue their most expansive dreams.

We print our books with soy-based ink on paper from sustainably managed forests. We power our Northern California office with solar energy, and we respectfully acknowledge that it is located on the ancestral lands of the Coast Miwok Indians. We also contribute to nonprofit organizations working to make the world a better place for us all.

Our products are available wherever books are sold.

customerservice@NewWorldLibrary.com
Phone: 415-884-2100 or 800-972-6657
Orders: Ext. 110
Fax: 415-884-2199
NewWorldLibrary.com

Scan below to access our newsletter
and learn more about our books and authors.